Everything You Know About England is Wrong

Everything You Know About England is Wrong

Matt Brown

BATSFORD

To Laurence and Tarah,
who probably know more about England than me,
despite not having lived here for a decade.

First published in the United Kingdom in 2019 by Batsford
43 Great Ormond Street
London WC1N 3HZ
An imprint of Pavilion Books Company Ltd

Copyright © Batsford, 2019
Text copyright © Matt Brown, 2019
Illustrations by Sara Mulvanny

ISBN: 9781849945233

A CIP catalogue record for this book is available from
the British Library.

25 24 23 22 21 20 19
10 9 8 7 6 5 4 3 2 1

Reproduction by Mission Productions, Hong Kong
Printed and bound by Interak Printing House, Poland

This book can be ordered direct from the publisher at the
website www.pavilionbooks.com, or try your local bookshop.

Distributed in the United States and Canada by
Sterling Publishing Co., Inc.1166 Avenue of the Americas,
17th Floor, New York, NY 10036

Contents

Introduction

'I have great respect for the U.K. United Kingdom. Great respect.
People call it Britain. They call it Great Britain. They used to call
it England, different parts.'
Donald Trump, 3 August 2018.

Nobody quite gets England, least of all the 45th President of the United States. It is a nation without a national anthem; a country but not a sovereign state. England is proud to have spread democracy around the world, and yet has no written constitution and no devolved parliament of its own. England's patron saint never visited the country, nor indeed, heard the name England. It is a country of contrasts, conflicts and counterexamples. Everything you know about England is wrong.

This is the seventh volume of my series addressing common myths and misconceptions. It comes at a time when English and British identities are in flux. Withdrawal from the European Union places the country in uncertain waters. Nobody knows what lies ahead. But it could also be argued that most of us don't really know what went before.

Even the most cherished facts about our country turn out to be dubious. Did Henry VIII really have six wives? Is the River Severn England's longest waterway? Are you sure you know how to pronounce Shrewsbury? England is a land of contradictions, crying out to be unpacked. *Everything You Know About England Is Wrong* seeks to do just that, and put a smile on your face.

My chief focus is England, but I do tackle wider myths where appropriate. For example, the Union Jack flutters on a flagpole of misconceptions. It is a British emblem rather than an English one, but does not seem out of place in a book about England. Conversely, I've shied away from myths that are specific to the capital. Anyone wanting to know why the Tower of London won't fall if the ravens flee, or why Big Ben *isn't* the name of the bell should seek out *Everything You Know About London Is Wrong*.

I've also avoided material on Britain's place within Europe. The Brexit process has suffered so many turns, twists and reverses that any attempt to cover it in these pages would be futile and quickly rendered out of date. This is primarily a book about culture and history, and so I've left the politicians from its pages. Except for Winston Churchill. And Donald Trump.

Some topics I will not tackle, because they are stupid, banal and obvious – better left to Internet listicles. Nobody thinks England is shrouded in fog anymore. The notion that nobody cares about food in England is dismissed by a casual browsing of daytime television. We don't all talk in Cockney rhyming slang, or have terrible teeth, or live off jellied eels and Yorkshire pudding. You won't find too many stereotypes in this book. Except for the British love of tea and scones ... because that's actually quite interesting.

As with every book in this series, the idea is to have a lot of fun while cocking a snook at received wisdom. The things we get wrong stick with us far more surely than those we get right, so don't be disheartened if a long-held 'fact' gets overturned or a squirrelled-away titbit turns out to be duff. To err is human and, in this age of encroaching Artificial Intelligence, we need to cherish our errant ways all the more.

So, turn the page, lie back and think of England. Or Britain. Or the UK. And let the nitpicking begin!

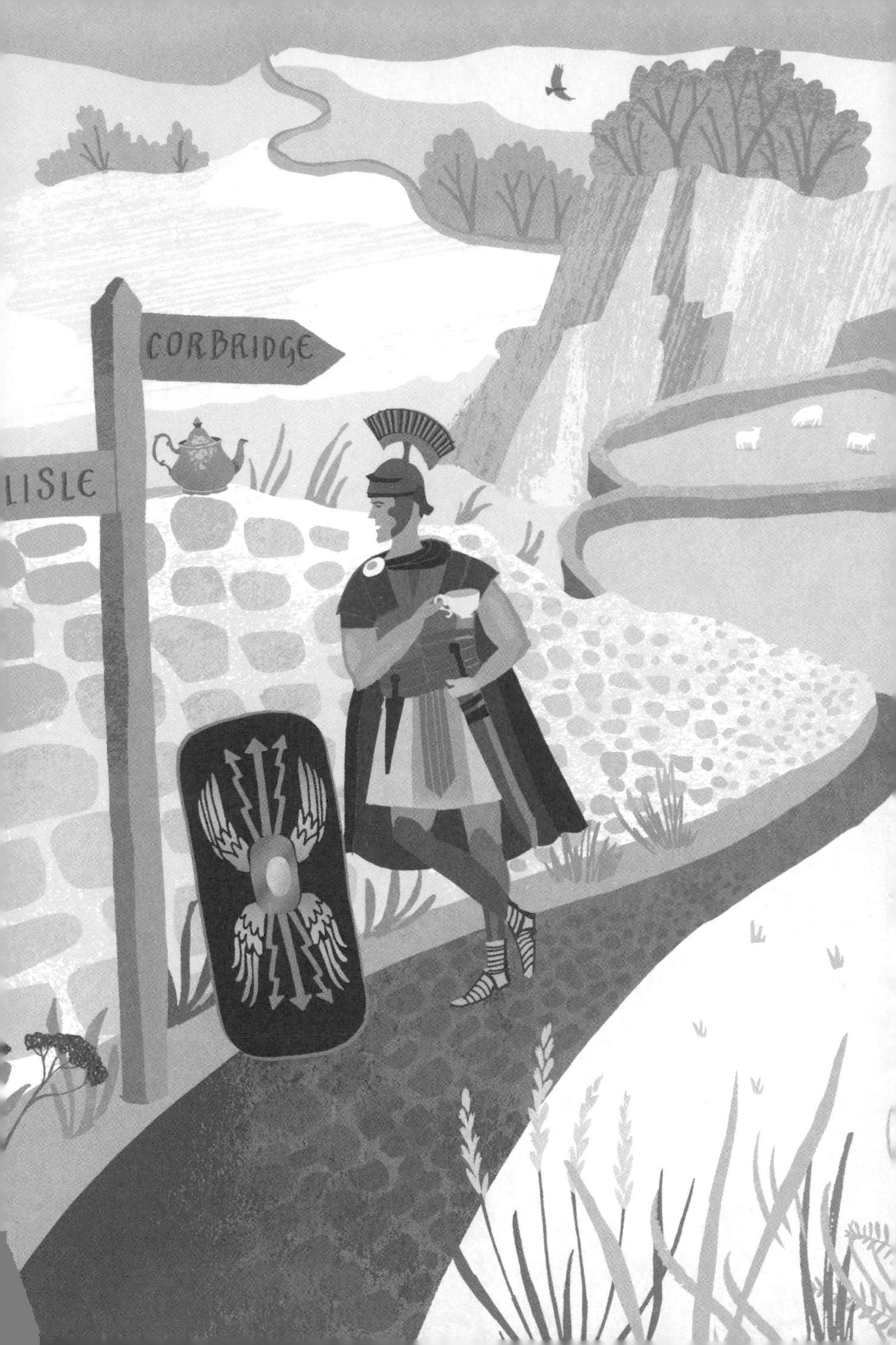
CORBRIDGE
LISLE

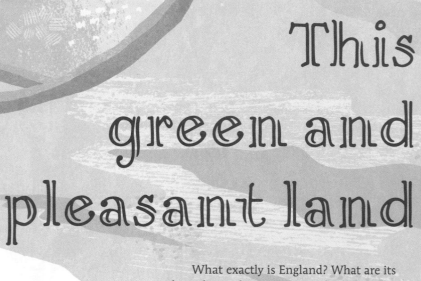

This green and pleasant land

What exactly is England? What are its boundaries, longest river and tallest building? Let's start with some definitions.

England, Britain and the UK are all the same thing

Why does the UK field English, Scottish, Welsh and Northern Irish football teams, but enter the Olympics as 'Team GB'? Why do international licence plate codes mark the country as GB and not UK? Is London the capital of England, Great Britain, the United Kingdom, or all of these? Ireland's not British, but it *is* in the British Isles – what gives?

The tangled web of territories is a constant source of confusion to outsiders, but also to residents and even authorities. When Ordnance Survey – the national mapping agency of the United Kingdom – published an online guide to the different terminology, it had to make at least two corrections after readers spotted errors. It's like explaining the offside rule in football: you might think you've got the basics nailed, but numerous details, exceptions and sensitivities must also be taken into account. Like a mad fool, I shall now attempt to unpick those differences.

Let's start at the top. The widest term people use, when prodding this part of the globe, is 'the British Isles'. The British Isles is usually intended as a geographic term, encompassing all the islands and territories off the north-west coast of France. England, Scotland, Wales, both parts of Ireland, the Isle of Man, the Orkneys, the Channel Islands ... if it's coloured green and surrounded by blue, it's part of the British Isles.

The term might be easy to understand, but it's loaded with political confrontation. Ireland was once a part of the United Kingdom, but achieved independence (as the Irish Free State) in 1922. Irish people may quite understandably wince at the phrase 'the British Isles'. It may be used with purely geographic intent, but it's hard to escape the suggestion of overlordship inherent in the adjective. Unfortunately, nobody has ever invented a satisfying alternative. Suggestions include 'The Isles', 'the Atlantic Archipelago' and 'the Anglo-Celtic Isles'. All of these come with their own problems. Careful writers and broadcasters tend to say 'the UK and Ireland' for most purposes.

Let's dig down to the next level. The British-Irish Isles (to use another alternative) contain just two sovereign states. These are the United Kingdom and the Republic of Ireland. The ROI is easy enough to understand. It comprises about four-fifths of the island of Ireland. The remaining one-fifth is Northern Ireland, which is part of the United Kingdom. To introduce a note of confusion even here, people from anywhere on the island may refer to themselves as Irish first and foremost, depending on political views and personal taste.

The United Kingdom unites four countries: England, Northern Ireland, Scotland and Wales. None of this quartet counts as a sovereign state, though the latter three have devolved law-making assemblies. The first whiff of a United Kingdom came in 1603, when James VI of Scotland inherited the English throne as James I. The countries then shared a monarch for 100 years until the Acts of Union (1707) merged them into a single state, the Kingdom of Great Britain. It wasn't until 1801 and union with Ireland that the phrase United Kingdom became commonplace.

You see how it's already getting a little complicated? Brace yourself, for we're now coming to the meat of it. Great Britain is the trickiest concept to get one's head around, and that's because it has two definitions. The first is geographic. Great Britain is simply the largest island in the region – the chewed-croissant of England, Scotland and Wales. Based on this meaning, places like the Isle of Wight and the Scottish islands (the croissant crumbs, should we pursue this weak analogy) are not part of the island of Great Britain. More commonly, though, Great Britain is used in its political context. Here, it's understood to mean anything that's part of the UK but isn't Northern Ireland.

Let's just recap by zooming out again. The nations of England, Scotland and Wales club together to form Great Britain. Add Northern Ireland and you get the sovereign state of the United Kingdom. Hang around with the Republic of Ireland, and we have the British Isles (or whatever politically neutral term you wish to use). And that's the crux of it, at least to beginner's level.

Already, I can hear people screaming 'What about the Isle of Man, you prat?'. What, indeed. This small island, about the size of Leeds, lies in the Irish Sea between Northern Ireland and northern England. It is a political anomaly. Mann (as it's more succinctly called, though note the double 'n') is not part of the United Kingdom or Great Britain*. It is a Crown Dependency, a possession of the British monarch, who holds the title of Lord of Mann. Residents of Mann are considered British citizens, with passports that say as much. However, the island has never been affiliated with the European Union. Its residents were never able to work in other EU countries without permits.

Two other Crown Dependencies lurk to the south of Great Britain. The Bailiwicks of Guernsey and Jersey – otherwise known as the Channel Islands – have a similar status to Mann. They are self-governing, and not part of the UK or Great Britain, but those who live there are considered British citizens. Smaller channel islands, such as Alderney and Sark, fall within one of the two bailiwicks.

We're almost there, but a final mention should go to 14 other territories around the world who claim a particularly close relationship to the parent country. These are the British Overseas Territories. Simply put, they are

---

* FOOTNOTE: Incidentally, the Isle of Man has one of the oldest continuous parliaments in the world. The Tynwald has existed for a thousand years or more – records are unclear. It is of a similar vintage to the Althing parliament of Iceland. I mention this because Westminster is sometimes known as 'the mother of all parliaments', even though it is nowhere near as long-standing.

fragments of the British Empire that never declared independence. Like the Crown Dependencies, they are not part of the United Kingdom, but rely on the parent state for defence and international representation, and also look to the British monarch as head of state. I say 'look to', but three of the territories have no permanent population to do any looking (British Antarctic Territory, British Indian Ocean Territory and South Georgia and the south Sandwich Islands).

The best known BOTs include Bermuda, the Cayman Islands, the Falkland Islands and Gibraltar. The most unusual is surely Akrotiri and Dhekelia on the island of Cyprus. The territory comprises three non-connected areas that live in messy cohabitation with Cypriot enclaves and the UN Buffer Zone that divides the island. It is the only territory under British sovereignty to use the Euro as its official currency.

So there we have it. What a dog's dinner of definitions. And, bear in mind that the careful, pedantic reader will perceive at least three inaccuracies. Nobody writing about this stuff ever quite gets away with it because many of the terms are open to interpretation and alternative readings. Even the authorities get bogged down in this nominative entanglement. Take 'Team GB', the brand under which British athletes compete at the Olympic Games. The term was adopted at the turn of the century to unite athletes from disparate sports. Critics point out, rightly, that the name alienates athletes from Northern Ireland, which is not part of Great Britain. Team UK would be a more inclusive term, but that doesn't sound nearly as pleasing to the ear. Besides, that brand would itself ignore potential competitors from the Crown Dependencies and the British Overseas Territories. Team UK+CD-BOT is hardly an option, at least until we start selecting artificial intelligences for competition.

Avoiding such absurdities is one of the many reasons I've decided to focus the majority of this book on England rather than Britain or the UK. You know where you are with England – a straightforward, well-understood country. Surely there's little scope for misunderstanding? ...

England was first settled at the end of the last ice age, 12,000 years ago

Before we get on to comfortable, familiar, modern England, we should first look back to the country's ultimate origins. For how long have humans strolled this green and pleasant land and called the place home? The intuitive answer, if you think about it, is to assume these lands were colonized at the end of the last ice age*, some 12,000 years ago. Before that time, much of the island was covered in ice sheets. It would have been a forbidding landscape both for humans and their prey.

Britain seems to have been bereft of inhabitants during this chilly period. Humans only arrived in numbers once the ice had retreated. The first settlers ventured over here 12 millennia ago or, to put it in more familial terms, during the time of your great-(x 500)-grandparents.

They did not need to construct boats or navigate the English Channel. With much water still locked up in ice at northern latitudes, sea levels

---

* FOOTNOTE: Technically, it never really ended and we are still living in an ice age. See *Everything You Know About Planet Earth Is Wrong* for more on that topic.

were lower than today. Britain was connected to continental Europe by a large plain known as Doggerland. Our ancestors simply walked across. Rising sea levels swept over this land bridge, but perhaps not as long ago as you might imagine. Britain eventually became an island about 6,500BCE, or 3,000 years before the earliest works at Stonehenge. Despite being cut off from the mainland – without so much as a referendum – the region we now call England remained populated right up to, including, and hopefully beyond the Brexit era.

Britain, then, has supported a permanent population for about 12,000 years. Yet there were still older 'Britons' who settled these isles long before. In fact, the human prehistory of Britain stretches much further back in time – almost a million years.

Over such unfathomable ages, the climate changed many times, from icy and uninhabitable to reasonably balmy. Whenever the ice retreated, people moved in. The earliest recorded humans were not of our species. Flint tools from Happisburgh* in north-east Norfolk have been dated to at least 814,000 years ago, possibly much older.

They were created by a species of human known as *Homo antecessor* – the first known inhabitants of England (and, indeed, Europe). No bones have ever been found but, amazingly, we have seen their footprints. In 2013, unusual tidal conditions in Happisburgh washed away a layer of surface sand to reveal the footprints of adults and children. Although now washed away, these were the oldest known human foot marks outside of Africa. They were heading towards what is now Great Yarmouth.

Other humans came and went over the millennia. The Neanderthals made it to Britain around 400,000 years ago. The town of Swanscombe in Kent contains a monument to their arrival. Here, a towering sculpture of a flint axe forms the centrepiece of a local nature reserve. It's not quite Jurassic

---

* FOOTNOTE: This is pronounced Haze-bro. The many bizarre pronunciations of English place names are a recurring theme in the book.

Park, though a plaque on the ground informs us that straight-tusked elephants once roamed around.

Britain seems to have been empty of humans between 180,000 and 60,000 years ago, when the Neanderthals returned. They were joined, then supplanted by modern humans about 40,000 years in the past. Their tenure was intermittent, as the climate turned first one way, then the other. At 12,000 years and counting, we are probably enjoying the longest spell of British habitation by modern humans. Long may it continue.

Land's End to John o' Groats is the longest distance in the UK

It's funny what a grip this epic journey has on the British imagination. Land's End in the extreme southwest of England and John o' Groats* at the northeast tip of Scotland mark the start and finish of a popular journey of endurance. People flock to the challenge for fun, charity or personal accomplishment.

It is tackled most often on foot, but others have accomplished the journey on skateboard, in a wheelchair, entirely on public transport, or on a unicycle. One brave soul – Sean Conway in 2013 – even completed a swim around the coast. Some walkers make the journey barefoot. At least two trekkers cross-dressed. One rambled naked. Another covered the distance on a hand-powered bicycle, while dressed as a gorilla. If an intangible journey between two places can ever be dubbed iconic, this is it.

With so many people making the pilgrimage, you might think the route and distance would be well defined. They are not. The traditional distance – the

---

* FOOTNOTE: Nobody seems to agree on the official formatting. The local tourism site sticks to John O'Groats while Wikipedia opts for John o' Groats. Visit Scotland chances its arm with both. In 2018, Cornwall Council decreed that Land's End should officially carry an apostrophe, ending decades of confusion.

one you'll find on the famous sign posts at either end – is 1,407km (874 miles). Choose your route carefully, though, and you can trim this down to 1,310km (814 miles). Nobody has yet made the journey by crow but, as that bird flies, the route is just 970km (603 miles). One man completed the route without leaving his living room. In 2016, Aaron Puzey used a virtual reality headset plugged into Google Street View to cycle the distance on an exercise bicycle. Conversely, many walkers would rather go off-road and take a scenic route. The more established paths can follow some 1,900km (1,200 miles). The options are infinite.

The two termini are also a bit random. Land's End in Cornwall* is indeed at the most south-westerly point in Britain, but the official visitor centre and signpost are in the wrong place. A more westerly spot can be found just to the north on the exceptionally named Dr Syntax's Head. Dangerous cliffs mean that the public cannot stand here. At John o' Groats the situation is still more dubious. Here, the visitor centre sits in the mid-curve of a bay, with more northerly coast on either side. It's patently obvious to anyone who visits that more northerly and easterly points exist. Many walkers carry on a mile or two to Duncansby Head, which looks a much better candidate for a north-east tip. You can get still further north by heading west to the Dunnet Head RSPB Nature Reserve.

---

* FOOTNOTE: While we're in the region, let's dispel another myth; 'Which English county has the longest coastline?' is a common pub-quiz question. The obvious answer is Cornwall, which is about four-fifths surrounded by sea. The quizmaster will then chuckle and reveal the answer as 'Essex'. According to Ordnance Survey – and there can be no higher authority on the matter – Cornwall is indeed the correct answer. It beats Essex by some 181km (112 miles) according to their measurement.

Hadrian's Wall marks the border with Scotland

If walking the *length* of the country, from Land's End to John o' Groats, seems a bit of a struggle, then walking the *breadth* is much easier. The pinched neck of England, where the coast-to-coast distance is shortest, coincides with the route of Hadrian's Wall. This Roman fortification stretches 117.5km (73 miles) from the Solway Firth in Cumbria to the mouth of the Tyne on the east coast. It is a trek of many contrasts, passing through suburbia, rural lands, rolling hills and floodplains. It cannot be done without gaining blisters, and I speak from personal experience.

Work on Hadrian's Wall began in 122CE. It took about six years. Though it cut across the most northern, windswept fringes of their empire, it represents one of the most remarkable feats of engineering ever undertaken by the Romans. Sadly, only about 10 per cent of the structure survives today.

Like just about every ancient structure on the planet, Hadrian's Wall is richly imbued with myth and fancy. The wall is so misunderstood that I'm going to break this one down into microfallacies.

Hadrian's Wall marks the boundary with Scotland

No, it does not. The wall never so much as kisses the national border at any point. It lies entirely within England. At its eastern end, the fortification is some 109km (68 miles) away from Scotland – about as far as Canterbury is from central London. True, it does cosy up to within a kilometre of Scotland at the western end, but this is a one-off, and as close as things ever get.

But it used to mark the boundary with Scotland, right?

Wrong. Hadrian's Wall has *never* marked the border. Look again at the eastern end. It passes through the middle of Newcastle. Plenty of England rises above that city, and always has. It's called Northumberland.

OK, but Hadrian's Wall did mark the boundary between Roman Britain and the barbarian north

The wall may have served as an emblematic frontier, but the reality was more nuanced. Roman soldiers regularly struck out and held territory farther to the north. The Antonine Wall is one example, constructed a generation after Hadrian's Wall. This turf fortification was some 161km (100 miles) north of its predecessor, but was only held for eight years. Before any of this, the Romans had established forts and camps into the foothills of the Highlands. Known as the Gask Ridge system, these fortifications only operated for a handful of years in the decades before Hadrian's Wall was constructed, but they show that the Romans didn't simply draw a line in the sand and refuse to cross it. A few suspected Roman outposts have even been discovered as far north as Inverness.

The wall was a military barrier to keep the barbarians out of Roman Britain

It was intended as a defensive feature, but only up to a point. The wall was not designed to repel a full-on assault or stand up to prolonged siege. Its forts were garrisoned with auxiliary troops rather than the serious fighting force of the legions. It probably served more as a symbolic deterrent – beyond this line, you are entering proper Roman territory, and we will deal with you. For much of the time, the wall's chief function was as a checkpoint, controlling the flow of trade, immigration and taxation.

It's the longest fortification in England

While Hadrian's Wall is considered the longest Roman artefact anywhere, it is not the most extensive fortification in England. For that, we have to turn to Offa's Dyke, which broadly parallels the Welsh border. The dyke – which comprises a ditch below an embankment – runs some 240km (150 miles), making it approximately twice the length of Hadrian's Wall (although it does have significant gaps). Its origins are sketchy. The dyke is conventionally attributed to Offa, King of Mercia from 757–796CE. Offa had the fortification built to protect Mercia from the neighbouring kingdom of Powys in Wales.

At least the name is correct. Hadrian's Wall was a wall

It included a wall, but the structure was much more complex than a simple stack of stones. Turrets, milecastles and forts punctuated it at regular intervals. A notable ditch – still visible in places – tracked the north side of the wall, while the south was followed by a military road, two continuous earthworks and a smaller ditch. To call it a wall is to describe New York's finest icon as the Staircase of Liberty.

But Emperor Hadrian was responsible for its construction?

He was! You'll be surprised by now to learn that at least one fact about the wall is true. Its construction was ordered by the Emperor Hadrian in 122CE during his visit to Britain. The idea might have been around at earlier times, but Hadrian had the clout to make it a reality. The name 'Hadrian's Wall' is, however, of more recent origin. We do not know what name was used by the Romans or their neighbours.

Hadrian's Wall

The River Severn is the longest waterway in England

The identity of England's longest river would seem unassailable – as solid a fact as might be found. At school, we all learn that the River Severn is the mightiest. It passes by Bristol and on through Gloucester, before wiggling deeper inland to Tewkesbury, Worcester and Shrewsbury as though seeking out those towns that foreigners struggle to pronounce. At 354km (220 miles) the Severn is slightly longer than the River Thames, which is officially 346km (215 miles). Londoners, accustomed to being first at everything, may sulk about this, but the Severn is England's longest river. No amount of nitpicking can change that fact.

Oh yes it can – and for two reasons. The first is easy to see on a map. While the Thames flows wholly within England, the Severn curls back on itself and heads into Wales. Its journey through the Welsh hills accounts for about one-fifth of its length. If we're talking solely about England, then, the Thames is the longest river by some margin. On that act of pedantry, the Severn remains the longest in the United Kingdom, but loses its boast about England.

A case can be made for the Thames even without paddling in the shallows of semantics, and here we must look for the source of the river. By tradition, the Thames begins at Trewsbury Mead, a remote meadow in Gloucestershire. This location is marked as the source on Ordnance Survey maps, and all guidebooks to the Thames start here. Don't expect to get your feet wet. The source of the Thames is a measly spring that only issues water after heavy rain. I've been; it's rubbish.

A much more convincing candidate can be found nearly 18km (11 miles) away near Cheltenham, where a small village known as Seven Springs lives up to its name. Here, down some steps beside an anonymous layby, one can find a hidden pool fed by seven dribbles of water. These natural springs are the source of the River Churn, a tributary of the Thames.

Seven Springs is in water all year round, unlike the fickle trickle of Trewsbury Mead. For reasons not altogether clear, though, the Churn is seldom counted as part of the Thames. Its waters do not contribute to the official length. Including this branch would add a further 22.5km (14 miles) to the Thames, and it would then outflow the Severn. No rational explanation can explain why the tributary from Trewsbury is favoured over that from Seven Springs. The choice was declared in the 16th century, and remains definitive, despite objections from an endless parade of killjoys like me. Having visited both, I'm wholeheartedly in favour of Seven Springs and an elongated Thames. But, then, as a man who writes about London for a living, I would say that, wouldn't I?

Incidentally, neither the Thames nor the Severn is the longest river within these islands. The River Shannon in Ireland, at 360.6km (224 miles), beats both its British rivals. That is, unless we add those extra miles of Churn onto the Thames, in which case, it triumphs again.

An English city must have a cathedral

What constitutes a city? In England, there is only really one way to tell. A city is a place that the monarch, or long tradition, has declared a city. No other criterion – the presence of a cathedral, university or decent coffee shop, say – is relevant.

We might suppose that a city is simply a large town. That works as a rule of thumb. Birmingham and Manchester are clearly cities; Pontefract and Mablethorpe are indubitably towns. It's not hard, though, to find munchkin cities that don't meet expectations. The City of London is England's smallest. With a resident population of 8,000 people and well-known dimensions of a square mile (it's actually slightly larger), it would be small even for a town. Over the border in Wales, the city of St Davids counted just 1,841 souls in the last census. It's practically a village. Compare these with some of England's largest towns – Reading (233,000), Dudley (195,000) and Northampton (189,000) – and we see that population size is no certain indicator of city status. More people live in Croydon (just one of 33 local authorities in London) than in the 11 smallest English cities combined. Croydon has never been granted city status, despite asking six times and containing several very good coffee shops.

Neither population nor size alone is good enough to establish somewhere as a city. So what about a cathedral? Received wisdom holds that the presence of a big church is a golden ticket to citydom. That was once true, and accounts for the special status of tiny places like St Davids, Wells, Ripon and Truro. All are seats of a Church of England Diocese (areas with bishops), and all have cathedrals. But the rule no longer applies. Fifteen English cities have no Anglican cathedral, including Cambridge, Leeds,

Nottingham, Sunderland and Westminster (the Abbey does not have cathedral status, while Westminster Cathedral is Catholic). Conversely, five English towns possess a cathedral but are not considered cities. These are Blackburn, Bury St Edmunds, Guildford, Rochester and Southwell.

Imposters can be found, too. The Hertfordshire towns of Welwyn Garden City and Letchworth Garden City are not, in fact, cities. Reading and Milton Keynes contain signage to the city centre when, technically, no such places exist. White City in west London is neither a city nor particularly white (the name comes from a series of marble-clad exhibition halls, called the Great White City, that graced the area in the early 20th century). London itself is of dubious status. It contains the City of London and the City of Westminster, but the wider area is not officially a city. Meanwhile, Guildford City Football Club have taken it upon themselves to promote their town's status to the next level.

England currently contains 51 cities, and the wider UK supports 61. The most recent is Chelmsford, granted city status in 2012 to mark the Queen's Diamond Jubilee. Similarly, Preston got the nod in 2002 as part of the Golden Jubilee. If the Queen is still with us in 2022, perhaps Croydon will finally get its wish at the seventh time of asking.

Southern England ends at the Watford Gap

In an age when making jokes about other nationalities can land you in hot water, the British tribes still trade jokes about each other with abandon. Scousers steal hubcaps; the people of Norfolk are inbred; the Scottish are thrifty and unhealthy; the Welsh are disturbingly fond of sheep; Yorkies are all outspoken whippet owners; the people of Grimsby reek of fish; and let's not get started on Essex.

The English, in particular, cultivate a higher order of regional stereotyping. We class people as either Northerners or Southerners (Midlanders are usually subsumed into one of these, or else entirely forgotten about). Either label comes with prejudices. Northerners are rough-and-ready, plain-speaking, hardy souls, quite prepared to visit a seafront nightclub in the middle of winter without first consulting the coat rack. Southerners, by contrast, are delicate creatures, effete and easily offended. They are self-absorbed and reluctant to talk to strangers, or even their neighbours. Northerners are painted as working class, while Southerners are of the bourgeoisie, and know how to spell it.

Where is this magical frontier, the national crease that bisects north and south? It doesn't exist, of course, but that hasn't stopped people trying to define it. One of the most common assertions is that the south of England ends at the Watford Gap. I would love to report that this is a formidable rift, separating the people like some fantastical Game of Thrones landscape feature. No. It is a service station on the M1. The 'gap' refers to low-lying land between two hills that also accommodates the West Coast Mainline and the Grand Union Canal.

The Watford Gap is nowhere near Watford – at least not the Watford everybody's heard of. The service station is named after a small village in Northamptonshire, and not the town beloved of Elton John. This is doubly counterintuitive because the famous Watford lies at the extreme north of the Tube map, so blinkered Londoners might readily assume that the benighted lands of the northerners lie just beyond. But no. You have to drive another 97km (60 miles) through the Home Counties to reach the Watford Gap services.

Why did this humble village and service station get a reputation as some kind of border town? A few reasons might be suggested. Because it's perched within a narrow gap between limestone hills, those travelling by narrowboat or stagecoach may have viewed it as a threshold; a physical gateway into the Midlands. A well-known coaching inn once thrived in the pass. It must have heard many an 'are we nearly there yet?' from impatient southerners

heading north, and vice versa. The gap also snuggles up to a linguistic division. Whether you say 'barth' (southern) or 'bath' (northern), 'larff' or 'laff' depends on which side of the line you grew up. None of this is a precise science, however. Any attempt to define a clear border between north and south is contrived and futile. A clip around the lug 'ole for the daft apeth wot tries it.

Watford Gap services, incidentally, once enjoyed a reputation for rock'n'roll glamour, as unlikely as that sounds. In the 1960s, when motorways still felt futuristic, the Gap was a thrilling place to take one's lunch. During tours, bands including The Beatles, the Rolling Stones and Pink Floyd stopped off for late-night meals at what was then known as 'the Blue Boar'. To say its star has waned would be an understatement. A 'load of old Watford', as fans of Cockney rhyming slang might review it.

The Shard is the tallest structure in the country

Rising 310m (1,017ft) above the Thames, the Shard skyscraper has dominated the London skyline since 2011. Almost three times the height of St Paul's Cathedral, the Shard is often touted as Europe's tallest building. It is no such thing. Three blocks in Moscow are loftier. The Shard is, at the time of writing, the tallest building in the European Union, but that crown is set to vanish with so many other precious items down the back of a Brexit-shaped sofa. Surely, though, the Shard must be the tallest structure in the country? Not even close.

The Shard can claim to be the tallest *building* in England or the UK. It stands more than 30m (around 100ft) over its nearest rival. If we're talking about *structures*, however, then the Shard barely skyscrapes into the top ten. A structure can take any form you care to name: a radio mast, a flagpole, a church spire, a teetering cylinder of mashed potato. Buildings, by contrast, must contain habitable floors – flat surfaces upon which one might stand and coo at the view. The Shard is champion of the latter category, but there are nine taller structures dotted around England.

The loftiest of all is the Skelton mast in Cumbria. At 365m (1,197ft), it's a whole Nelson's Column taller than the Shard. The Belmont mast in Lincolnshire was once even taller at 385.5m (1,264ft) – higher than the roof of the Empire State Building in New York. This has since been lopped back somewhat, putting Belmont into second place. When other communications masts around the country are taken into account, the Shard turns out to be only the tenth tallest structure in the country. Still, I'm not convinced as many tourists would pay to climb up an exposed radio mast in Cumbria.

Milton Keynes is awful

Nowhere on Earth, with the possible exception of Croydon, provokes as much casual snobbery as Milton Keynes. The Buckinghamshire town, another wannabe city, has a reputation for concrete repetition, windswept plazas, identikit service roads and boring modernity. 'Bland, rigid, sterile, and totally boring,' reckoned Francis Tibbalds, president of the Royal Town Planning Institute. Millions have perpetuated this opinion, without ever visiting (or wanting to visit).

Milton Keynes is sometimes described as the third generation of new town. The wheeze of building brand-new conurbations in the middle of nowhere began at the turn of the 20th century with Ebenezer Howard's 'garden cities' of Letchworth and Welwyn (neither are actually cities). A second wave came immediately after the Second World War when towns such as Basildon and Stevenage sprang up around existing and suddenly bewildered villages of the same name. Milton Keynes did not trouble most atlases until the late 1960s, when an unremarkable settlement was subsumed into the much larger newcomer along with Bletchley, Wolverton, Stony Stratford and numerous other villages. It was to be bigger, bolder and griddier than any new town before or since.

Milton Keynes is all about the transport. The M1 runs next door, and fast trains from London take half an hour. The car dominates, of course. Three great avenues stretch the length of the new town, regularly punctuated with car parks. Named Avebury, Silbury and Midsummer Boulevards, they nominally evoke the distant past. Indeed, the central boulevard was purposely aligned to meet sunrise on Midsummer's Day. The effect is ruined – and this is so Milton Keynes – by the subsequent construction of a shopping centre bang in the middle of the alignment. But Milton Keynes is also embracing the future of transport. You might, for example, glimpse a driverless pod car, undergoing trials along the town's invitingly wide 'redway' pavements. Electric buses are common, while every one of the copious car parks has electric charging for vehicles. Cycle hire racks stand on many corners. Even the shopping centre has internal transport, thanks to an ersatz steam train that pootles round the concourse. It's as though the place has one foot in the past and one in the future, while the present is trapped in some kind of intermediary region.

There's much to deride in Milton Keynes, but also much to admire. It has the country's largest indoor ski slope. Twenty million trees beautify the urban area. Public art is everywhere. That shopping centre includes the most delightful novelty clock, designed by Kit Williams. People are moving here in record numbers. A quarter of a million souls now call Milton Keynes home where, just half a century ago, this was nearly all fields. The economy is roaring. In 2015, the town had a higher growth in jobs than any other major town or city in the UK. Expansion plans are moving apace. Clearly, Milton Keynes is not awful.

Why do we sneer at such towns? It perhaps has something to do with British character. A love of the old that trumps the shine of the new. England never really embraced the grid system. The boulevards of Paris and the regimented blocks of New York are alien to our sensibilities, which favour radial roads from a central core. The City of London, for example, still follows a medieval street plan, with lanes and alleys twisting off in unpredictable directions, despite the forest of skyscrapers overhead. Many of the suburbs, a product of more recent centuries, have leisurely curves built in, like country lanes, rather than a criss-cross of roads and avenues*.

---

* FOOTNOTE: There are exceptions, of course. View Marylebone or Soho from above and it's right angles as far as the eye can see. Pimlico, too, is built on a grid – albeit a demented grid with acute angles and random side streets. Areas like this do not have the same charm as twistier neighbourhoods like Southwark, Wapping and Hampstead. At least not to me.

New towns fly in the face of tradition. They offer long, straight roads built with the motor car in mind. Yet they also come with their own attractions, if only we have the willingness to see them. How can you not admire the concrete cows of Milton Keynes? Who wouldn't want to drive around Hemel Hempstead's 'magic roundabout' – six mini-roundabouts in hexagonal orbit around a central parent? Besides, reputations change. One hundred years from now, when the motor car is but an historical curiosity, tourists will flock to Milton Keynes, Harlow and Stevenage for a glimpse into a quaint past, much as today we venerate York, Chester and Norwich. I'll buy you all a holo-pint if I'm wrong.

Around the counties

In which we find a misconception for all 48 English counties.

Every county has stories, stereotypes and superstitions that, on closer scrutiny, are built on foundations of dung. This section explores at least one dubious tale from every county. For the purposes of this list, I've chosen to focus on the 48 ceremonial counties (also known as geographic counties), rather than the 39 'historic counties' that would have included largely defunct entities such as Huntingdonshire, Westmoreland and (dare I say it?) Middlesex.

Bedfordshire is snoresville: Somehow, somewhen, Bedfordshire got a reputation as England's most boring county. Perhaps it's the name, with its somnolent qualities. Or maybe it's the reputation of the largest towns – Luton, Bedford and Dunstable are absent from most people's bucket list. In many travelogues of England, Bedfordshire is either ignored or slandered. Even the 'Experience Bedfordshire' tourist website describes its subject matter as 'often overlooked'. But this is also a county of many beauties. To the south, the chalk hills of the Chilterns offer majestic views over the county plain. Dunstable Downs (with its tree cathedral) and Whipsnade (of zoo fame) hold particularly stunning aspects. This is the county that gave the world Ronnie Barker, John Bunyan, Ian Nairn, Monty Panesar, Carol Vorderman, Paul Young and Ben Whishaw. Luton Carnival is the largest one-day carnival in the country. Bedfordshire has also been home to seismic historical events. Henry VIII's marriage to Catherine of Aragon was annulled at Dunstable Priory, a split that precipitated England's break from Rome and centuries of political and religious turmoil. A big deal. Besides, people of this county have the best nickname: Clangers! Bedfordshire deserves to be celebrated and this is why I've put it at the top of the list (also for alphabetical reasons).

Berkshire has an architectural joke: Windsor is a town full of historical quirks and curiosities – from its crooked house, to a peculiar statue of Elizabeth II and her corgis, to the country's only pavement clock. And that's before we get inside the castle. Most curious of all, though, is a persistent myth about the architecture of its second most prominent building. Visit the Guildhall today and you'll not only enjoy an excellent local museum, but you'll also be invited to look up at the porch roof. It would appear that the Tuscan-style columns do not quite reach the ceiling. In jauntier words, they abort short of the porch they purport to support. Christopher Wren, the architect of the Guildhall, thought these inner columns were unnecessary. The local burghers begged to differ and insisted on their inclusion. In mockery, Wren made the columns a little too short to prove his point. It's a good story but, without any documented evidence, the myth is itself unsupported. In fact, the columns do reach the roof by means of tiles that are smaller than the capitals, and hence can't be seen from below.

Bristol's literary pub: Bristol is both a city and a county though, perhaps surprisingly, it is only the sixth smallest county by population. Among its many glories is a fine old pub known as the Llandoger Trow. This unique and peculiar name comes from the Welsh village of Llandoger noted for manufacture of trows, a kind of cargo boat that once sailed the River Severn. The pub is twice blessed with nautical literary connections. It was here, so tradition holds, that Daniel Defoe met Alexander Selkirk, the one-time castaway who inspired *Robinson Crusoe*. The Trow was also influential on Robert Louis Stevenson while writing *Treasure Island*. He supposedly modelled the Admiral Benbow pub from that story on the Llandoger Trow – some say he even wrote his most famous novel in the pub. Alas, neither tale is backed up by firm evidence. Until the 1930s, the location of the Defoe-Selkirk summit was usually given as the Star Inn, or else a house in St James's Square, both elsewhere in Bristol.

Buckinghamshire's misnamed town: As we've already seen, the much-maligned new town of Milton Keynes is in dire need of myth and urban legend, if only to make it feel a little more lived in. One of the few examples concerns the name itself. Hearsay would have us believe that the town borrows the surnames of writer John Milton and economist John Maynard Keynes. It's not clear why these two men, with little or no connection to Buckinghamshire, should be so honoured. In fact, the name of Milton Keynes is ancient. A nearby village had been enjoying that moniker (or close variants) since at least the 13th century, taking its name from the de Cahaignes family from Normandy, who held the local manor. The village has since adopted the name Middleton to distinguish itself from the new town.

Cambridgeshire's vanished coastline: I must apologize to the good people of this region for personally misrepresenting the lie of their land. I've long cultivated a bit of a side hobby for map-making. In 2013 I was asked to draw a map of Anglo-Saxon England for Patricia Bracewell's novel *Shadow on the Crown*. I sketched out the country, confidently appending labels for the various territories such as Mercia and Wessex, but I made a bit of a blooper when it came to the outline. I began my map by tracing a modern chart. But the coastline has changed considerably over the past 1,000 years, especially in what we now call Cambridgeshire.

The county today is entirely landlocked but, until about 400 years ago, much of the northern section was under near-permanent flood. The region known as the Fens is close to or below sea level. Most of this area was uninhabitable during the medieval period. Had a map been drawn at the time, it would have shown the waters of the Wash sweeping much farther inland. Hence why we still say the 'Isle of Ely' when referring to the high ground around that small city, even though it's now surrounded by farmland. The Fens were drained in the 17th century, and the coastline pushed outward. Elsewhere in England, of course, the coastline has shrunk due to erosion (see Suffolk, below, for a notorious example). Any modern-day map of Britain seeking to depict the country of a thousand years ago should really take these changes into account.

Cheshire's murderous bylaws: Chester clings on to its past like few other English cities. Much is either medieval, or dolled up to look medieval. One can circumnavigate the city atop the medieval city walls – the most complete surviving example in the country. This persistence of history extends to the city's bylaws. According to the *Metro* website, a Welshman may not enter Chester before the sun rises, and he must scarper, too, before sunset. It gets worse. Any inhabitant of Chester may shoot a Welshman if he spies one within the city walls after midnight (but only if it's a Sunday, and a crossbow is used). The article, written by the curiously prolific '*Metro* Web Reporter' on 27 April 2009, is not alone in credulously presenting this strange rule as fact. It was even raised in the House of Commons as recently as 2007. The edict does have an historical source. In the early 15th century, the future Henry V got into a bit of a spat with the Welsh, and forbade them from entering Chester (a border town) between certain hours, on pain of death. There is no record of any Welshman ever suffering retribution. Nor was the local law ever repealed as far as anyone knows. Even so, the medieval intolerance has long been superseded by other laws, not to mention a persistent state of peace between the English and the Welsh (at least off the rugby field).

On another local sporting note, Chester Football Club's ground straddles the national border, with the entrance in England but the pitch in Wales. This makes them the only professional English team who play their home games in another country. (Berwick FC, in case you're wondering, play in the Scottish leagues, but from English soil.)

The City of London's growing square mile: The ancient centre of London was first laid out by the Romans almost 2,000 years ago. It's tiny – by far the smallest plot of land to carry the status of a ceremonial county. Nicknamed 'the Square Mile', the City really did cover that area – well, a fraction over 1 sq. mile (2.7sq. km) – for much of its recorded history. Thanks to expansion in the 1990s, though, it has now swollen to 1⅛ sq. miles (2.9sq. km). In recent years, the City's cluster of skyscrapers has begun to push out into surrounding territories, leading some to speculate about further expansion. The Square Mile sobriquet may yet get more inaccurate.

Cornwall's famous foodstuff: The Cornish pasty is a delightful treat that wraps an infernally hot filling of beef and veg inside a folded circle of pastry. Other variations, vegetarian or filled with cheese, are technically just 'pasties', and not of a Cornish persuasion. The savoury snack is protected by EU regulation and must be baked in Cornwall to be sold under that name (although it's not clear how long this can last post-Brexit). Tempers flared hotter than a pasty filling in 2006 when historical research suggested an origin in Devon and not Cornwall. A recipe found in Plymouth pre-dated anything Cornish by some 200 years. Another blow came in 2015. A food historian pointed out that traditional Cornish recipes tended towards the vegetarian – miners and agricultural labourers could not afford a daily parcel of beef. The meat-filled variant that is today given protected status was first concocted by a London-based cookery teacher who also invented the phrase 'Cornish pasty'. In truth, the deliciously simple recipe of meat and veg in pastry probably had a number of independent origins.

County Durham's French monkey: Pity the people of Hartlepool. When anybody remembers the town at all, it is usually to mock their ignorance in hanging a monkey. During the Napoleonic wars, local lore tells us, a French ship was dashed to pieces off Hartlepool in a storm. The only survivor was a monkey, the ship's mascot. The people of Hartlepool had neither seen nor heard a monkey before. The hairy, babbling creature, unable to answer their questions, was mistaken for a Frenchman and hanged as a spy. Needless to say, no primary evidence of the incident exists. The first known mention comes decades later in a popular song by Ned Corvan, which may have been nicked from a similar Scottish folk myth. The people of Hartlepool, though, are able to laugh at themselves and the legend. The spurious monkey is a common emblem or mascot at local sporting clubs. It even has a statue.

Cumbria's missing lakes: The most north-westerly county is best known as the home of the Lake District. The idyllic corner is poorly named as it contains just one lake – Bassenthwaite Lake. All the other large bodies of water are styled as meres, waters and tarns. This includes 'Lake Windermere', which is tautological (a 'mere' being a type of lake), and should properly be known simply as Windermere. None of the fake lakes are particularly impressive by world standards of size. The largest (Windermere) could fit into Lake Ontario (smallest of North America's Great Lakes) 1,283 times, in terms of surface area. Their beauty, though, is indisputable and an endless source of inspiration for poets, painters and writers.

Derbyshire's typo: It's difficult to spend much time in this delightful county without hearing tales of the Duke and Duchess of Devonshire. Their noblenesses preside over 14,500ha (36,000 acres) of land (an area roughly the size of Sheffield), and inhabit Derbyshire's crown jewel, Chatsworth House, like a pocket royal family. But why does the Duke of Devonshire own so much of Derbyshire and not, you know, Devon? An old story puts it down to a clerical error. Supposedly, a scribe mistakenly wrote 'Devonshire' rather than 'Derbyshire' on the official papers of ennoblement and the name stuck. As with so many of these stories, the facts are long lost to history but there is certainly no evidence for such a blunder. The Chatsworth website says the title was chosen simply because it was vacant, whereas the Earl of Derby was already in use. This raises new questions, however. An Earl of Devon was also active, hence the adoption of 'Devonshire'. So why not take Derbyshire when only Derby was active?

Devon's wild ponies: Devon is known for its wild ponies, so iconic of Dartmoor that a pony appears on its National Park logo. The hardy animals have roamed these hills for thousands of years. Any would-be pony thieves should beware. None of the 'wild' animals is truly wild – all are owned by somebody. Visitors are encouraged not to approach the ponies, and feeding is forbidden by bylaw. Also, Devon is sometimes said to be the only English county to have two separate coastlines. This is doing a disservice to Merseyside, whose Birkenhead and Liverpool moieties are only joined up via Cheshire (though you can, of course, take the famous ferry or one of two tunnels). Now, speaking of famous coastlines ...

Dorset's Jurassic Coast: The Jurassic Coast attracts visitors from all over the world, thanks to its stunning clifftop walks and famous fossil beds. The coast played such an important role in the history of paleontology that it now carries the status of a World Heritage Site. But the name is something of a misnomer. While fossils from the Jurassic era are readily found along the coast, it is equally blessed with layers from the Triassic and Cretaceous. The Jurassic Coast could, more accurately, be named the Mesozoic Coast – this being the collective term for the three periods represented in the cliffs – but then it would lose an attractive resonance with a certain movie franchise.

East Sussex's Home Guard: You won't find Walmington-on-Sea in your maps app, and yet half the population of England will know roughly where it lies. Walmington – somewhere near Eastbourne – was the setting for the fondly remembered BBC comedy series *Dad's Army*. The show caricatured the Home Guard, a Second World War reserve fighting force drawn from volunteers who could not serve in the regular armed forces. On TV, this was a bunch of loveable if ineffectual old men, by turns doddery, incontinent or officious. The real Home Guard no doubt included its share of puffed-up Captain Mainwarings and flappable Joneses, but they were not representative of the typical recruit. Many of the volunteers were in the prime of life. Young men with occupations crucial for the war effort, including farmers, railway workers and utility workers, were exempt from conscription. Up to 50 per cent of some Home Guard units were men in their twenties. Others were still too young to join the regular armed forces. These included future politician Tony Benn and astronomer Patrick Moore, who both joined the Home Guard as teenagers. The older volunteers wouldn't have been pushovers, either. Many served in the First World War and knew their way around a rifle.

Essex's unlikely warrior-king: Was one of Scotland's most famous kings born in an Essex village? Robert the Bruce (1274–1329) is noted for securing Scottish independence from England, and for taking inspiration from a persistent spider. He is not, generally, regarded as an Essex Boy. Yet a long-standing legend places his birth in the village of Writtle near Chelmsford. The evidence is circumstantial, but tantalizing. The Bruce family certainly held land in the area and were regular visitors. Robert even got married there in 1302. We know that, about a month after Robert's birth, his father was in London for Edward I's coronation. Did he take his whole family too? Were they staying in Writtle when the famous son was born? It seems unlikely that the heavily pregnant mother Marjorie would have made the cart or horseback journey down from Scotland, though it's possible they made the trip in the spring and enjoyed a prolonged stay in England. In the absence of solid evidence, we can only speculate, but his ancestral home of Turnberry Castle in Ayrshire seems more likely.

Gloucestershire's infamous regicide: Despite its situation in the groin of England, Gloucestershire is among the prettiest counties. It includes much of the Cotswolds and Forest of Dean. As though to balance that attractive exterior, Gloucestershire also boasts a famously brutalized posterior. The deposed Edward II was supposedly killed with a red-hot poker during his imprisonment at Berkeley Castle in 1327. This was no mere stab to the back. The sizzling iron was forcibly inserted into his majesty's anus on the orders of his own wife, Queen Isabella. It's impossible to imagine a more painful way to go. Happily, these blistering events probably never happened. No recorded evidence for the gruesome act exists. Accounts from the time vary in the manner of death: some say illness, some suffocation or strangulation, and one chronicler even has Edward fleeing to Italy to spend his remaining days in a hermitage. Death by seared intestines is just one among a selection of fates. The red-hot poker appears to be hearsay that, owing to its gruesome character, has outperformed rival stories and survived down the centuries into modern accounts.

Greater London's existential crisis: Everyone knows that London is the capital of England and the UK, but what exactly is London? Does it even exist? It's surprisingly difficult to find a place with that name. We have Greater London (the ceremonial county), Inner London, Outer London, the City of London (another, much smaller, ceremonial county), and the City of Westminster – all of which have formal definitions. But just 'London'? The name occurs in the titles of various roles and organizations like 'Mayor of London' and 'London Fire Brigade', but these are really shorthands for Greater London. One of the few examples where London is a *bona fide* geopolitical term is as a European Parliamentary constituency. Unfortunately, the UK's promised withdrawal from the European Union will have a regrettable side-effect: London will cease to exist.

Greater Manchester's cursed statue: In 2013, Manchester Museum made global headlines because of an 'ancient Egyptian curse'. A miniature 4,000-year-old statue of a man named Neb-Sanu was on the move. Each day, the statuette would partially rotate, despite its tamper-proof enclosure in a glass cabinet. Many dismissed the story as just another fatuous 'curse-of-the-mummy' yarn without any basis in reality. But this one was different. Time-lapse video footage showed, beyond doubt, that the statue did indeed turn on the spot. What was going on? Far from an ancient curse, the exhibit's motion was caused by vibration from passers-by and traffic outside. Neb Sanu has a convex base like a Subbuteo player, which allowed him to turn, while his flat-bottomed cabinet-mates behaved as statues should. Still, the spooky mystery boosted visitor numbers to the gallery, so some good came from the fake curse.

Hampshire's maritime myths: Portsmouth is home to HMS *Victory*, that magnificent and well-named ship that led the fleet during Britain's trouncing of the French and Spanish navies at the 1805 Battle of Trafalgar. Upon its decks, Admiral Lord Nelson drew his last breath several hours after receiving a bullet wound. One of England's greatest heroes, Nelson is an absolute spank-magnet for made-up facts. Chief among them is his eyepatch. The admiral was never known to wear such an item. His right eye was blinded in conflict, but not disfigured. He had no need for a patch, and only gained one in heroically embellished portraits after his death. Everyone knows his last words to be 'Kiss me Hardy', an imploring command to the captain of the *Victory*. Notes from the battle confirm that he made the request (fulfilled, but only a peck on the cheek). His true last words came some time later and are recorded as the far more worthy, 'God and my country'. Another famous vessel at Portsmouth, the *Mary Rose*, comes with its own myths. Henry VIII's flagship supposedly sank on her maiden voyage in 1545. In fact, she launched 34 years before that in 1511, fought in several wars, and was an ageing veteran when she sank in the Solent while repelling the French fleet.

Herefordshire identity crisis: I scratched around for the longest time trying to find a well-known misconception about Herefordshire. It is a small county, at least in terms of population. With just 191,000 people, only the City of London, Isle of Wight and Rutland are less populous. So I started asking friends: 'What do you know about Herefordshire?' More than one person gave me a puzzled look and said 'Is that in Wales or England?'. They're clearly not alone. Type 'Is Herefordshire ...' into Google and '... in England or Wales' materializes as the top autosuggest – a measure of common search queries. For the record, Herefordshire is most definitely and wholly in England and has been for centuries. We have to go back some 1,600 years to find the land under Welsh control. But, like most borderlands, some commingling is inevitable. Welsh culture and language pervade the county infinitely more than in, say, Kent. Also, do not confuse the county with Hertfordshire. They differ by just one letter.

Hertfordshire's misplaced studios: I have the pleasure of living in this county, right next door to Elstree Studios. The view from my bedroom window is frequently enlivened by long queues for *Strictly Come Dancing* and other shows. As I type these words, I'm watching technicians construct a fake Buckingham Palace for use on *The Crown*. But the studios have a bit of an identity problem. The place is often billed as 'Elstree Studios, London', when it's quite patently in Hertfordshire. More seriously, it's not even in Elstree. Wrong side of the tracks. This is good old Borehamwood. To add to the confusion, a second Elstree Studios, owned by the BBC, can be found down the road, much to the consternation of Uber drivers who head out this way for the first time. The BBC Elstree Studios are home to the long-running soap opera *EastEnders*, set (obviously) in the East End of London but again filmed in Hertfordshire. A similar misnomer blights the studios in nearby Leavesden, home of the *Harry Potter* films. The venue is a major attraction, marketed as the Warner Bros. Studio Tour London. Lazy tourists might be put off were they to associate the boy wizard with Hertfordshire, so London it is. By way of bonus movie fact, the hallowed ground where the *Star Wars* films were shot is now the Borehamwood branch of Tesco. In a juicy, possibly deliberate coincidence, the freezer section is built on the exact spot that once housed the set for the Ice Moon of Hoth. Yoda's swamp is now a petrol station. The force is strong in pump 12.

The Isle of Wight's invitation to the world: Could every single person in the world fit onto the Isle of Wight? It's one of those factoids that gets recirculated every now and then – but has anyone checked the maths? It's not hard. The Isle of Wight covers 380sq. km (147sq. miles). That's 380 million sq. m (more than 4 billion sq. ft). The population of the world is currently 7.6 billion people (UN estimate, June 2018). Divide people by area and you get an answer of 20 people per sq. m. Cosy, to say the least. The factoid was once true, about a century ago when the world population was much smaller, but today would require some spectacular human pyramids.

Kent's fallacious fauna: 'There'll be bluebirds over the white cliffs of Dover,' promised Vera Lynn in one of her signature wartime songs. Sadly, the bird is not indigenous to the British Isles. The American lyricist who penned those words – coincidentally called Walter *Kent* – was unaware.

Lancashire's beefy fib: This north-westerly county has one of the most delicious myths in this book. According to local legend, James I was dining at Hoghton Tower, near Preston, when he was presented with a particularly tasty cut of loin. So impressed was the king that he decided to bestow a knighthood upon the choice piece of beef. 'Arise, Sir Loin,' he supposedly proclaimed, simultaneously creating the world's first sirloin steak. Needless to say, there is no primary source (or sauce) for the august victual's anointment. More likely, the name comes from the French *sur-loin* for 'over the loin'.

Leicestershire's crooked king: Leicester's most famous inhabitant is both new and very old. Richard III made unexpected headlines in September 2012 when his long-lost remains were discovered beneath a local car park. They put paid to the myth of the king as a lumbering hunchback, 'not shaped for sportive tricks'. The skeleton showed curvature of the spine, but not in a way that might have caused a noticeable crookback. The withered arm of stage and screen was not apparent. Rather than a shuffling cripple 'cheated of feature by dissembling nature', the king was an able swordsman who had died in battle fighting his enemies (the last English king to do so).

Lincolnshire's flat reputation: This eastern county is often dismissed as boringly flat. Anybody who's explored its only city would object to that label. Lincoln is centred on a prominence of back-breaking gradient – the main route up to the castle is known as Steep Hill. Further east, the Lincolnshire Wolds offer a chain of hills that out-peak anything else on this side of the country between Yorkshire and Kent. Further, Lincolnshire had the world's tallest building from 1311 to 1549 in Lincoln Cathedral. In more recent times, the Belmont telecommunications mast was once the tallest structure in Western Europe. Lincolnshire certainly has its high points, despite the reputation.

Merseyside's Scouse heritage: Many a myth persists about the good city and citizens of Liverpool. Only a few Liverpudlians have curly hair and moustaches. Very few are inclined to steal your car's hub caps. But it's the regional nickname – the Scouser – that holds the best story. The demonym derives from an inexpensive meat-and-veg stew called scouse that was once a popular midday meal for sailors at the port. It would be wrong to assume, as many do, that Scousers invented the dish after which they are named. The stew was originally imported from Norway or northern Germany where it is known as *lobscouse*. Sailors all over Europe partook of this simple hotpot, but it seems to have been unusually popular among those from Merseyside. Nor is the term particularly old. Dockers in Liverpool may have referred to each other as Scousers since the 19th century but it was only during the Second World War that the word spread to outsiders. Newspaper articles from the 1940s typically place the word in quotation marks. Several accounts describe the phrase as navy slang, suggesting it was the mobilization of Liverpudlian sailors that brought the term to widespread attention.

Norfolk's artificial landscape: The Broads National Park is one of the most cherished natural landscapes in England. Unfortunately, it is neither a national park, nor entirely natural. This expanse of rivers and lakes is protected under a 1988 Act of Parliament but has never been granted the National Park status under which it markets itself. We should also remember that this is an artificial landscape. The unique progression of waterways were a side-effect of human engineering. Medieval workmen gouged out the basins and channels while excavating peat for fuel. Rising sea levels flooded the peat works, creating the pleasant landscape we see today. Not that any of this should detract from the Broads. It is a truly enchanting part of the country to explore, regardless of its status or genesis.

Northamptonshire's interplanetary trouser press:
The Corby trouser press, beloved of hotel rooms, has nothing to do with the town of Corby in Northamptonshire. It is named after John Corby, founder of the company who produced the gadget from 1930 at premises in Windsor. The town of Corby does, however, have an impressive namesake: a crater on Mars. Supposedly, the crater got its name in honour of a back-and-forth between the crew of Apollo 11 and mission control about current world news. The final item relayed to the crew concerned the World Porridge-eating Championships in Corby. Astronaut Michael Collins quipped that Buzz Aldrin might win a future event: 'He's on his nineteenth bowl.'

Northumberland's ongoing war with Russia:
The Wikipedia page for Berwick-upon-Tweed includes a dedicated section – unexpected for a small town of little note on the world stage – called 'Relations with Russia'. It addresses one of the more curious legends in English history: that Berwick is technically still at war with the state of Russia. The notion arose thanks to Berwick's status as a border town, which swapped between England and Scotland several times. Because of its fickle allegiance, the town was sometimes afforded special status in official documents. Specifically, the declaration of war against Russia in 1853 was reportedly given the stamp by 'Victoria, Queen of Great Britain, Ireland, Berwick-upon-Tweed and all British Dominions'. In the peace treaty that ended the Crimean War in 1856, Berwick was accidentally left off and, hence, remained at war with Russia.

It turns out there is little truth in the story. Berwick was once singled out (along with Wales) for special mention in official documents, but the anomaly was corrected in an Act of 1746. A century later, and neither the declaration of war nor the peace treaty mentions Berwick at all. I've traced the wheeze back to 1914, when the *Berwick Advertiser* recounts the story in the words of an Archdeacon Cunningham of Cambridge University. The Archdeacon concludes by saying he hasn't inspected the relevant documents to confirm the truth. The joke only grew from that point and came to a head in 1966 when the London correspondent of *Pravda* visited Berwick to sue for peace. The story was widely reported in the press, cementing the legend for another generation. 'Please tell the Russian people through your newspaper that they can sleep peacefully in their beds,' joked the Mayor.

North Yorkshire's rose-tinted history: It was one of the bloodiest chapters in English history. The Wars of the Roses pitted the armies of York (white rose) against those of Lancaster (red rose), a bitter struggle for the crown that lasted 30 years. Only it didn't quite happen like that. Nobody at the time thought of this as the 'Wars of the Roses'. That name was coined by Sir Walter Scott in his 1829 novel *Anne of Geierstein*, 350 years after the event (though earlier phrases like 'the Quarrel of the Two Roses' can be found). Nor was it a continuous slog of sword and butchery. The 30-year span of the conflict included long periods of peace, including a 12-year cessation between 1471 and 1483.

Most surprisingly, this was not a conflict between the cities of York and Lancaster*. The Lancastrian forces were more strongly associated with Gloucestershire and the Welsh borders, while the Yorkist faction was based in the south-east. Even the roses are something of an exaggeration. Nobles of the House of York did use a white rose as a symbol, but it was one of several (Richard III's most famous sigil, for example, was the white boar). The Lancastrians did not use the red rose as an emblem until after the conflict. Had you approached a combatant at the time and asked him 'How are the Wars of the Roses going for you?', he'd have given you a blank stare. The association with roses grew after the triumph of Henry VII. His marriage to Elizabeth of York was symbolized by the Tudor Rose, a white rose for Yorkshire on a red rose for Lancashire. The link was reinforced by Shakespeare more than a century later. In *Henry VI, Part I*, leading nobles from the two houses pluck their respective roses from a thorn in Temple Gardens. It is an entirely fictitious scene that, probably more than any other account, has contributed to our rose-tinted spectacles about the period.

---

* FOOTNOTE: A struggle still perpetuated by the respective universities of those towns in an annual sporting competition. York, my *alma mater*, always fields the best team.

Nottinghamshire's ancient tree: The Major Oak in Sherwood Forest is surely the most famous tree in England. The girthsome *Quercus* is said (without evidence) to have sheltered Robin Hood and his merry men during the 12th or 13th century. It's certainly old enough. Estimates range up to 1,000 years. Yet it's not, as often assumed, the oldest tree in the UK. Many yew trees are much older. The record is usually ascribed to the Fortingall Yew in Perthshire, which is reckoned at 2,000–3,000 years old. (Dating a living tree is surprisingly hard – you can't just cut it down and count the rings.)

Oxfordshire's insistence on Latin: While most counties are content to use sensible abbreviations – 'Berks' for Berkshire, 'Lancs' for Lancashire, for example – Oxfordshire shortens to 'Oxon'. There is no 'n' in Oxfordshire, yet one magically appears whenever it's abbreviated. The peculiar diminutive comes from *Oxonium*, the Latin name for Oxford. Why is that not a surprise? Other counties with unexpected shorthands include Hampshire (Hants), Northamptonshire (Northants) and, weirdest of all, Shropshire (Salop). All derive from older variations on the county name.

Rutland's Lilliputian claims: England's smallest county. Or is it? According to an episode of the BBC's *QI*, the tiny territory loses its title twice a day to the Isle of Wight. The two are of similar land area – Rutland just edging it – but, at low tide with more beach exposed, the island county overtakes its landlocked rival. It's a dubious claim, to say the least. County boundaries are fixed and do not wax and wane with the tides. Further, Rutland and the Isle of Wight are only the smallest if we're talking about historic counties. In terms of *ceremonial counties*, the modern patchwork of geographic counties I've used as the basis for this list, then both the City of London and Bristol are much smaller.

Shropshire's purloined cheese: Few English cheeses are as distinctive to the eye as the Shropshire blue. The deep yellow and blue dairy item is easy to spot in a crowded deli counter. Yet its connections to the West Midlands county are dubious at best. The cheese was first created some 650km (approximately 400 miles) away in Inverness in the mid-1970s – the first new British blue cheese for centuries. Originally marketed as Inverness-shire blue, it later adopted its familiar name in an effort to boost sales. Today, a small amount of Shropshire blue is made in its namesake county, though most comes from Leicestershire or Nottinghamshire.

Somerset's tiny city: 'Wells in Somerset is an ancient cathedral city in the picturesque district of Mendip,' says the Wells City Council website. No argument there. 'It is known as England's smallest city,' it continues. This is also true, thanks to some crafty wording. For Wells is *known* as the smallest city, even though it isn't. The City of London covers just over half the area of Wells and has a population that is 2,500 people fewer. It often gets dismissed as 'not a proper city' and lumped in with the much-wider area of London, but it is a *bona fide* city (and county) in its own right. Two even smaller cities – St Davids and St Asaph – can be found in Wales.

South Yorkshire's green lungs: The largest settlement in the area, Sheffield, has a reputation as a grubby place of work, toil and industry. But only among those who have never been. While it's true that the city was once an industrial powerhouse of smoking chimneys and vast steel works, today it is one of the most pleasant cities in England. Indeed, Sheffield claims to be the greenest city in the country, with 80 public parks and 650 other green spaces. Meanwhile, the Winter Gardens, recently built in the heart of the city, are a jaw-dropping mix of plant life and human engineering – said to be the largest urban glasshouse anywhere in Europe. With an estimated 2 million trees, the city supposedly has more per person than any other UK city (though this is difficult to verify).

Staffordshire's field of the dead: Lichfield, arguably one of England's more obscure cities, has found slightly wider fame through a myth about its etymology. Could Lichfield be built on a 'field of the dead'? The name suggest so. A 'lich' is an Old English word for a corpse (hence the lych gates that lead into the graveyards around churches). The area was particularly replete with corpses around 300CE, when the Roman authorities suppressed local Christians. A thousand were slain and their bodies left to rot in the open air, giving us the field of the dead. An area of land north of the cathedral carried the name Christian Fields until recent times, and images of scattered body parts were once part of the city's emblem. It all seems to fit. Proper historians, though, pooh-pooh the story. The city probably gets its name from the Old English for a pasture ('feld') beside a grey wood ('lich'). A gory meadow is far more evocative than an ash wood, however, and the legend persists.

Suffolk's lost capital: Stand on the cliffs of Dunwich and you might just hear the maudlin clang of bells; a ghostly toll from beneath the waves. This once-thriving town has gradually slipped into the sea. Dunwich was once a regional capital, home to 3,000 souls at the time of Domesday Book in 1086. Medieval storm surges and coastal erosion ate away at the old town and it was all but abandoned. Today, fewer than 200 people live in the area. At least eight churches have been lost to the sea over the centuries, the most recent in 1922. The bells may still be down there, but there is no possibility of hearing them toll. Even if the clangers are still attached, decades in the submarine environment will have rendered them mute by encrustation.

Surrey's most important signature: Question: Where did King John sign Magna Carta? Answer: At the bottom. It's a joke retold by generations of school children. The less whimsical answer is, of course, Runnymede, a water meadow beside the River Thames near Staines. That's not right either, though, as any pedant will tell you. Medieval kings did not sign important documents; they *sealed* them. A £2 coin, minted in 2015 to celebrate 800 years of Magna Carta, fell into the trap of showing John wielding a quill. Rather, he signified his royal assent by slapping a beeswax seal on the document.

Tyne and Wear's famous beer: During the 1990s, Newcastle Brown Ale was the most widely distributed alcoholic drink in the United Kingdom, reinforced by a highly visible sponsorship of Newcastle United FC. It still sells well, but no longer seems like the alluring, fashionable drink choice of my student days. Sure, I've moved on, seduced by the amber tide of craft ales. But Newkie Brown has moved on, too, and way out of Newcastle. In 2005, the brewery crossed the river to Gateshead, to much local disgruntlement. Five years later it made the next leap, leaving Tyneside for Tadcaster, North Yorkshire. The brand is now owned by Heineken and brewed in the Netherlands. Let me repeat, because I don't think many people realize this: Newcastle Brown Ale is not brewed in Newcastle, or even England. Some bottles now carry a 'Made in Holland' declaration, right above a geographically perplexing picture of the Tyne Bridge. The beer's reach has changed, too. Once seen as a working-class drink for northern England, it now sells most bottles in the USA as a rather fashionable tipple promoted by Liz Hurley.

Warwickshire's dubious sporting history: The famous event that catapulted a certain Warwickshire school's name to the far corners of the globe is marked thus on a plaque:

> 'This stone commemorates the exploit of William Webb Ellis who with a fine disregard for the rules of football as played in his time first took the ball in his arms and ran with it thus originating the distinctive feature of the rugby game. AD1823'

It does so with a fine disregard to both punctuation and historical evidence. Nothing from the time records Ellis's anarchic handplay. Indeed, the legend seems to be unrecorded before the 1880s – after Ellis's death – and even then, rests upon the anecdote of one Old Boy, who wasn't even present. I'm not saying it's wrong or untrue, but we only have hearsay to go on.

I suspect the truth is more nuanced. The rules of football were not codified at the time of the supposed incident, and some variations allowed handling. Ellis may have played a part in nudging the boys of Rugby toward a catching and throwing game, but the evolution no doubt took more twists than a greased scrum half.

The name of the school was immortalized at a later date after local leatherworker Richard Lindon manufactured the first ovoid balls for the boys. The shape won fans and became a standard part of the game in 1892. Ellis, who went on to become a noted man of the cloth, never recounted his contribution to the game, if it ever happened. He would, no doubt, be surprised to learn that he is considered the founding father of an international sport, which itself would help shape other games such as American and Aussie-rules football.

The West Midlands' answer to Venice: Ask anyone to give you a fact about Birmingham, and they'll probably quote the old adage that the city has more miles of canal than Venice. I was all geared up to debunk this stat but – surprisingly – it turns out to be true. According to Birmingham City Council (admittedly, they might be biased), the city enjoys 56km (35 miles) of canal, while Venice can only muster 42km (26 miles). The aquatic tourist magnet is, however, concentrated into a much smaller area than Birmingham's sprawling urban smear. Per square mile, Venice still triumphs, and may have some kind of quality versus quantity case. Brum also performs splendidly when it comes to green spaces. The city with a reputation for ugly concrete urbanism boasts more parkland than any other city in Europe. One wonders why it still has an image problem.

West Sussex's tide-turning king: Bosham might just be the most important village that no one has heard of. Its church appears, and is named, in the Bayeux Tapestry. It was in Bosham that Edward the Confessor and Harold met before heading to see William of Normandy for a very important chinwag about the Succession. Here, too, may lie the remains of King Harold (see page 106 for that discussion). The town also has close connections with King Cnut (spelled Canute by those fearful of unfortunate typos). The king of the Danes, Norwegians and English was such a powerful man that his courtiers believed he could turn the very tide by issuing a command. To show his limits, the king stood at the water's edge and ordered the waves to retreat. They did not, and the legs of the credulous assembled were soaked. Cnut's demonstration of his humility is one of the earliest recorded debunkings in English history, and so certainly deserves a place in this book.

The story is itself often misunderstood, with Cnut painted as an arrogant king who thought he held a power that only God could command. We still use the phrase 'turn back the tide' today as a metaphor for vainly attempting to stop the inevitable. The earliest accounts, though, make it clear that the king welcomed his dousing as a display of piety. Did the episode take place at Bosham? Half a dozen other places claim the legend, including Southampton, the Thames at Westminster and the Lincolnshire town of Gainsborough (on a tidal stretch of the River Trent). The first account of the myth came 100 years after the supposed events, and no location is given. In all probability it never happened, but once a good story is unleashed, even the will of a king can't stop it.

West Yorkshire's cardboard fairies:

Did fairies really prance before the camera of two Bradford schoolgirls? In five famous images, a troupe of tiny figures, dubbed the Cottingley Fairies, dance in the foreground while the two girls look on. To the modern eye, weary of digital manipulation and photoshopped images, the clear answer is 'no'. The supernatural beings are about as convincing as Donald Trump's press team. Yet many people were duped in the early 1920s when the photographs first circulated. Chief among them was Arthur Conan Doyle. With contrasting judgment to his super-rational creation, the Sherlock Holmes author thought the fairy images were credible. The case was debated for decades until, in old age, one of the Cottingley girls admitted to fakery. It is perhaps the most notorious practical joke of the 20th century.

Wiltshire's misunderstood landmark: To Stonehenge and the realm of the Druids. As Spinal Tap put it, 'nobody knows who they were or what they were doing'. We do know what they *weren't* doing, and that's building Stonehenge. The earliest incarnation of the circle is thought to date back to at least 3000BCE, while the great standing stones were put in place by Bronze Age Britons sometime around 2500BCE. The Druids, meanwhile, didn't arrive on the scene until the coming of the Celtic people around 500BCE. These European newcomers would have found the stones already ancient. The gap of centuries is as large as that between our own era and the Roman Empire. The Druids doubtless made use of Stonehenge, but they certainly didn't build it – despite what you might have learnt from comedy music films.

Engineers of the 1950s have as much claim to erecting Stonehenge. The great circle was extensively reworked during this decade. Fallen sarsens were lifted back into place and wonky stones were made true. If you take the opportunity to visit Stonehenge up close on the summer solstice, take a good look at the bases. Many of the stones are secured in place with concrete supports, some rather obvious.

Finally, although Stonehenge gave its name to henges in general, it isn't itself a true 'henge'. The technical definition requires an internal ditch, whereas that at Stonehenge is external. Woodhenge in Wiltshire and Seahenge in Norfolk also fail this test.

Worcestershire's saucy export: Were you, for some reason, to plan out a book about English misconceptions, you might draw up a list of quintessentially English items: tea, bowler hats, scones, umbrellas ... that kind of thing. I think I'm qualified to say that Worcestershire sauce would appear on that list. Not only is the savoury additive enjoyed by millions of Brits a year, but it also carries a most English name. Bizarrely, though, the greatest consumers of the brown condiment are not the good folk of Worcestershire. The sauce finds its largest audience in El Salvador, whose people eat it with (and as) relish. Because the name is essentially unpronounceable outside the UK, locals refer to the sauce as *la salsa Perrins*, after manufacturers Lea & Perrins. According to *The Wall Street Journal*, El Salvadorans get through 450 tonnes of the stuff per year.

Yorkshire, East Riding's anomalous name: Have you ever visited Hull, the UK's 2017 City of Culture? I grew up in the nearby town of Grimsby, from where we looked across the Humber towards Hull with suspicion. As well we might because, technically, Hull is not a city but a river. The town's full name is Kingston-upon-Hull. Unpacked, that means the city of Kingston built on the banks of the River Hull. To call it just 'Hull' is like referring to Shakespeare's birthplace as 'Avon', or naming the original home of Newcastle Brown ale as 'Tyne'. But they do things differently in Yorkshire, and Hull it remains. Perhaps 'Kingston' feels too recent. Most cities gained their names in Anglo-Saxon times, but Kingston-upon-Hull is a Johnny-come-lately. Until 1299, the small village at the confluence of the Rivers Hull and Humber was known as Wyke. In that year, Edward I took a shine to the place (supposedly after a hare led him to the spot), bought the land, and renamed it King's-Town. Everybody has called it Hull ever since.

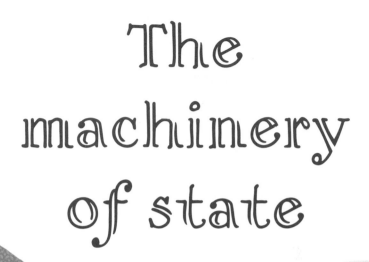

The machinery of state

Can the Queen become an atheist? Does it matter if the Union Jack flies upside down? And can a shop refuse your Scottish bank notes? Some surprising answers await.

The monarch is not allowed to vote, and other royal restrictions

Pity Elizabeth II. The nation's longest-serving monarch has spent her life in the company of politicians and lawmakers. Her signature must appear on every Act of Parliament before it becomes law (she has signed more than 3,500). And yet the Queen cannot influence the course of the process. As her own website says, the monarch 'has to remain strictly neutral with respect to political matters, [and is] unable to vote or stand for election'.

That 'unable' is a weasel word. No impediment in law bars the monarch from casting a vote. The Queen abstains in accordance with tradition and protocol, not because there's a bit of parchment somewhere saying that she mustn't. (Who, after all, would have authorized such a law?) It might be considered unconstitutional, and it would certainly stir heated debate in the media, but her vote would be valid. For the same reason (and possibly others), you will never hear the Queen declare that 'One is not amused at the policies of the Conservatives' or 'One sympathizes with the views of that Nigel Farage fellow'. Any hint of a political stance would be minutely scrutinized in the press. This custom of avoiding politics and polling stations is also expected of other senior royals, particularly those high up in the line of succession.

Can the monarch be an atheist? The situation has never arisen, at least not to public knowledge. Intrigue would ensue. British monarchs also head up the Church of England and adopt the title 'Defender of the Faith'. The Act of Settlement (1701), still in force, states that the line of succession will only tolerate Protestants. It's not clear, though, what would happen if a reigning monarch suddenly lost faith altogether.

It would certainly strike an odd chord – like a vegetarian chairing the Beefsteak Appreciation Society – but it may be manageable. An openly atheist monarch might just get away with it, so long as he or she agreed to respect the traditions of the church and not rock the boat. After all, much of the sovereign's role involves participation in ancient protocols and ceremonies that bear no reflection on the incumbent's personal views. Further, the Coronation Oath does not ask for belief, only that the monarch maintains and preserves the connections between the Protestant church and the state. It's all about business as usual, rather than business with enthusiasm. On the other hand, a bellicose irreligionist* would assuredly trigger a constitutional crisis.

Times are changing and even the rules governing the monarchy are not immutable. In 2013 the Succession to the Crown Act finally allowed for members of the royal family to marry Roman Catholics without ejection from the line of succession. However, the Act did not remove the bar on Catholics taking the Crown itself. Even after all these centuries, the idea that Britain's head of church and state should bow to the Pope remains decidedly unpalatable.

The monarch has one final and unique restriction. He or she is not permitted to enter the House of Commons on any pretext (except, one hopes, an emergency evacuation of a neighbouring room). The rule dates back to the mid-17th century when Charles I stormed into the Commons and attempted to arrest five MPs. Ever since, the monarch has been barred and must be represented by Black Rod. The state opening of Parliament, initiated by the monarch, takes place in the House of Lords.

---

* In case you're wondering, Richard Dawkins and the current Queen are 15th cousins, twice removed, according to his own genealogical research. He is as far down the line of succession as you or I.

The monarch's role isn't all barricades and obstacles. She might not be able to vote or turn Catholic or shout at the Prime Minister across the Commons, but the Queen does enjoy many privileges that even other royals can't access.

Immunity from the law: All criminal prosecutions are carried out in the name of the reigning monarch. He or she cannot be brought to trial for this would amount to an absurdity: The Queen versus The Queen. In addition, the monarch cannot be forced to give evidence in a trial. The latter scenario has been tested. In 1911, George V was falsely accused of bigamy. His Majesty was prepared to break with tradition and turn to the courts for redress, offering to take the stand if necessary. The attorney general ruled that it would be unconstitutional for His Majesty to give evidence in his own court. The monarch also enjoys total immunity from prosecution. Technically, the Queen could turn to a life of moped theft, or spend her days taking rifle shots at commoners from her balcony, and nobody could stay her hand short of a revolution. In reality, the merest whiff of regal wrongdoing would cause a media storm and constitutional crisis.

Power to appoint a Prime Minister: We live under the assumption that whoever commands a majority in the House of Commons will be sworn in as Prime Minister. It is not necessarily so. The monarch is responsible for the appointment. If the Queen so decided, she could shoo out the expected leader and appoint her kennel hand or stable boy. In practice, monarchs tend to shy away from such behaviour for the reasons of political neutrality we touched on earlier.

Exemption from tax: The monarch is exempt from paying most taxes. The present Queen has, however, made voluntary contributions to income tax and capital gains tax since 1992.

Grant a pardon: Did you hear about the two prisoners who were granted a royal pardon for saving a man from a wild-boar attack? The whole thing sounds positively medieval, but it happened at a Welsh prison in 2001. The men had their sentences reduced by a month after they intervened to save the life of the prison farm manager. The sovereign has the power to change the sentence of any convicted person, although the paperwork is usually, as in this example, delegated to the Lord Chancellor. The most high-profile modern case of royal pardon came in 2013, when computer pioneer, Bletchley Park codebreaking expert and all-round hero Alan Turing was granted a posthumous pardon for his 1952 conviction for gross indecency (as consenting to homosexual acts was then considered).

Drive without a licence: The monarch is the only person in the country who requires no driving licence to take a vehicle onto public roads. Nor does she need to display number plates. The present Queen learned to drive back in 1945, 13 years before the first motorway opened. Although she is normally chauffeured around in public, the Queen was still occupying the driver's seat into her nineties on her private estates.

Claim your sturgeon: In the unlikely event that you ever catch a sturgeon in British waters, you should either place it back in the water unharmed, or send it to the monarch. Sturgeon, along with whales and arguably dolphins and porpoises, are counted as Fishes Royal (even though three out of four are mammals), and are the property of the monarch. The same is true of unmarked swans.

The monarch's official home is Buckingham Palace

Every British monarch since Queen Victoria has made Buckingham Palace their chief London residence. It is the building most intimately associated with the Crown. Were you to say that you'd been 'invited to the Palace for a cup of tea', everybody would assume you meant Buckingham Palace. And that you are a liar.

Buckingham Palace, though, is not considered the official residence. If the Queen were to fill out one of those online forms that asks for a full name* and address, she would cite a much older building just off The Mall.

St James's Palace – a Tudor mansion built on the site of a leper hospital – is home to the royal court and serves as the formal residence of the King or Queen. Foreign ambassadors are received by the Court of St James's, not by Buckingham Palace. St James's Palace also plays an important role in the Succession. When a monarch dies, a group of bigwigs known as the Accession Council huddles together to confirm the name of the successor.

---

* FOOTNOTE: Elizabeth Alexandra Mary Windsor, in case you're wondering. Her full title, 'Elizabeth II, by the Grace of God, of the United Kingdom of Great Britain and Northern Ireland and of her other realms and territories Queen, Head of the Commonwealth, Defender of the Faith' is not included in most drop-down menus.

That name is then pronounced from the Proclamation Gallery, a crenellated balcony overlooking the public-facing courtyard of the palace. It is from this space, and not Buckingham Palace, that the official announcement of the next monarch shall be made. At the time of writing, St James's* is rarely used as a residence for the monarch, though the Princess Royal does have an apartment here, and the Prince of Wales shares a garden via the adjacent Clarence House.

Another, more blatant, myth about Buckingham Palace (and other royal residences) concerns the status of the flag. Hang around the gates for long enough, and you're sure to overhear someone say 'Look, the Union Jack's flying, so the Queen must be at home.' On the contrary, a fluttering Union Jack means that the monarch is *not* in residence. The Royal Standard – that red, yellow and blue confection adorned with lions and unicorns – is the one to look out for. Now, the observant pedant may be trying to score another point from this last paragraph, so I guess we better address the matter of the flag next ...

---

* FOOTNOTE: Note the 's on St James's; it is incorrect to say the Court of St James.

The Union Jack should be called the Union Flag when not at sea

This, this, THIS, dear reader, is the ultimate plaything of the pedant. Nothing* is more likely to wake a nitpicker from his slumbers (and it is usually a he) than to point at the national flag fluttering over a town hall and call it a Union Jack. 'I think you'll find,' you will at once be advised, 'that it's only a Union Jack when flown at sea, on a ship. When raised on a building, it should be called the Union Flag.'

Well, I've looked, and I don't find that, thank you. First off, the Union Jack's career as Britain's national flag is merely a custom. No law, Act of Parliament or Royal Decree ever established its status or its name. We may call it the Union Jack, or the Union Flag, or Winston Churchill's Multicolour Hanky, or anything we like, and we are not at odds with officialdom.

Next, the Flag Institute – which describes itself as the UK's national flag charity – notes that the Jack versus Flag distinction is a recent one. Before the mid-20th century, the flag was near-universally referred to as the Union

---

* FOOTNOTE: With the possible exception of calling the most famous tower in Westminster Big Ben. See the previous volume *Everything You Know About London Is Wrong* for a thorough discussion on why that peccadillo isn't as clear-cut as many a pedant believes.

Jack, whether on land or boat. Seek out mentions in any archive you care to name, and you will find that politicians, essayists and editors all refer to the Union Jack without any nautical context. It was, and is, the commonly established name for our national flag.

It is a useless distinction in any case. Why should a flag change its name just because it has gamely ventured out onto the water? OK, I know boating types like to have alternative words for everything – starboard for right, stern or aft for back, decks for floors, splice the mainbrace for whatever the hell that means*. And the term 'jack' *is* used to denote small flags at the front – sorry, bow – of a ship. But the whole point of a national flag is its universality. It should be recognized and understood by everyone. Why muddy the waters by having two names? Plus, 'the Union Flag' stinks as a name. It's bland and generic and could apply to any group of united territories. Union Jack is unique and internationally recognized as a hallmark of Britain.

That brings us on to the most serious error concerning the Union Jack, and that is to fly it upside down. I say 'serious', but there is only one consequence of doing so: you will anger another cohort of pedants. People get greatly exercised by this kind of thing. 'Sir – I was disgusted to notice that the Union Jack flying over the Town Hall in celebration of St George's Day was being flown upside down,' wrote one livid reader of the *Banbury Guardian* in 1950. 'I was flabbergasted to see our victorious troops in North Africa hauling down the German flag and replacing it with the Union Jack, which is not only allowed to lie on the ground but is eventually hoisted upside down!', bewailed an anguished cinema-goer to the *Liverpool Echo* in 1942 after watching a news reel. Many other examples can be found in the newspaper archives; it is a pet subject of the kind of people who like to write letters to editors. Incidentally, every example I can find from the mid-20th century (and there are many) refers to the Union Jack and not the Union Flag, again showing how *that* piece of pedantry is very recent.

---

* FOOTNOTE: As you can tell, I don't sail very often. Somebody else will have to write *Everything You Know About Boats Is Wrong*.

For the record, a correctly flown Union Jack should have a thick white band touching the top of the flag on the side attached to the flagpole. Tradition has it that an upside-down Union Jack is a symbol of distress. If that ever were the case, it is no longer a sensible way to seek help. Far better to wave your arms about and look distressed than to carefully orient and raise a flipped Jack in the hope of attracting a passing flag geek.

We shall finish – in an upside-down way – by going back to the flag's origins. It might be assumed that the Union Jack was created at the formation of the United Kingdom to join together the national flags of England, Scotland, Wales and Ireland. That's not quite right. Indeed, it's quite wrong.

Like the United Kingdom itself, the flag evolved piecemeal and, in elementary form, pre-dates the UK. The first version was dreamed up in 1606 shortly after the Kingdoms of England and Scotland found themselves in strained alliance under the person of King James (the first in England and the sixth in Scotland). The modern flag combines the St George's cross of England, the blue saltire of Scotland and the red saltire of Northern Ireland, but contains no direct reference to the Welsh flag. Curiously, the blue of the Scottish flag does not match that in the Union Jack. Since 2003, the Scottish saltire has been fixed as sky blue, or Pantone 300. The blue of the Union Jack, meanwhile, is a deeper shade of Pantone 280.

The royal family are the epitome of Englishness

Among the clichés and stereotypes that serve as shorthands for Britain, the Royal Family reign supreme. Visitors to the country can't get enough of the Windsors, and all the pomp they engender. One only has to witness the crowds who form daily for the Changing of the Guard at Buckingham Palace or Windsor Castle; ceremonies that don't even feature the royals themselves. Meanwhile, every tourist gift shop is well-stocked with cardboard face masks of the Queen; souvenir mugs of William and Kate or Harry and Meghan; and the occasional dusty portrait of Prince Charles. Nothing shouts 'England' more than the Royal Family. Funnily enough, no English dynasty has inherited the throne in a thousand years.

To find a monarch with several generations of English blood, you have to go back to the time of King Harold. The last Anglo-Saxon king, killed in 1066, was a scion of the House of Wessex, a dynasty that had ruled England (with Danish interludes) since the 6th century. The Anglo-Saxons, of course, came from Germanic stock, but by Harold's time they'd had four centuries to settle down and turn themselves into the indigenous English. The same cannot be said of subsequent royal dynasties.

House of Normandy (1066–1154): French. William the Conqueror and his immediate successors were from Normandy in north-west France. A variant of French was the official language of court for most of the Middle Ages.

House of Plantagenet (1154–1485): Further French. The Gallic flavour continues, with English kings hailing from Le Mans (Henry II), Bordeaux (Richard II) and Rouen (Edward IV). Early members of the dynasty held impressive chunks of France, and spent much of their time there.

House of Tudor (1485–1603): Welsh: The Plantagenets and their cadet branches (York and Lancaster) were put to bed by the Wars of the Roses, when a victorious Henry VII assumed the throne. Henry was Welsh – at least through his father's line. Nobody at the time referred to a 'House of Tudor'. The phrase was coined by David Hume in the 18th century, but is now ingrained.

House of Stuart (1603–1714): Scottish then Dutch. The first Stuart king, James I, was also known as James VI on account of his pre-existing thronecraft in Scotland. William III later seized the crown from the feckless James II (and VII). He was Dutch. So Dutch that he went by the name of William of Orange. He reigned jointly with Mary II, who was a daughter of James II and, hence, the Stuart rule continued a little longer.

House of Hanover (1714–1901): German. This family, mostly called George, came over from Hanover on the death of Queen Anne. The debutante George I couldn't speak English for much of his reign. Four Georges in a row (two of whom were born in Hanover) were enough to give this period of history its common name of the Georgian era. Victoria was its last representative.

House of Saxe-Coburg and Gotha (1901–17): German. With the death of Victoria, Edward VII assumed the throne and the time of this most foreign-sounding dynasty (named from his father's lineage) had come. But not for long. This house still reigns securely, but the Germanic name was changed in 1917 for reasons you can probably guess.

Today, we recognize the House of Windsor (1917–2066*). Our current royals are undoubtedly English, but recently descended from everywhere except England.

---

* FOOTNOTE: When, to round off 1,000 years since the Conquest, the royal family decides to abolish the line of succession. The next king or queen is chosen via a holographic reality TV show in which would-be monarchs must attempt to withdraw a sword from a stone. It could happen.

Notwithstanding my footnote, how long will the Windsors continue to occupy the Britannic throne? It might not be long. The past two dynastic shifts – Stuart to Hanover and Hanover to Saxe-Coburg Gotha (Windsor) – were a consequence of the Crown passing through the female line (Anne and Victoria). The male bias of genealogy saw to it that the subsequent monarchs took their father's dynastic titles, and a change of house ensued. Were Prince Charles to stick strictly to patrilineal lines, he would inherit the throne as a member of his father's dynasty. He and his successors would reign as the House of Schleswig-Holstein-Sonderburg-Glücksburg.

This is unlikely to happen. The royal family has, in recent years, relaxed its archaic rules of inheritance. Since 2013, male siblings no longer take precedence over female siblings when it comes to succession. A first-born daughter now trumps a fourth-born son, where previously (as with Princess Anne) that was not the case. Similarly, Charles is likely to go along with the spirit of the age and continue with his mother's name. Besides, the quadruple-barrelled Teutonic alternative (or even its shortened form as the House of Glücksburg) would strike an awkward note in post-Brexit Britain. Then again, the town of Glücksburg is on the Anglia Peninsula near the Germany–Denmark border – from where the invading Angles originated some 1,500 years ago. We've come full circle.

'God Save the Queen' is the English national anthem

Nothing could feel more official, more establishment than 'God Save the Queen'. The ploddy, deferential anthem is sung at any occasion of national importance, from state banquets to football internationals. It is the national anthem of the United Kingdom (and several Commonwealth countries), but not of England, Scotland, Wales or Northern Ireland individually.

This leads to an oddity. When lining up for big football matches, the Scottish sing 'Flower of Scotland' and the Welsh use 'Hen Wlad Fy Nhadau'. Neither is an official national anthem, but both are established by long tradition. The English, by contrast, plump lazily for the wider British anthem on most occasions.

As national anthems go, 'God Save the Queen' is peculiar for a number of reasons. First, and most obviously, the lyrics must change periodically to match the gender of the ruling monarch. When Queen Elizabeth II finally passes on the regal baton to the current Prince of Wales, a sixth of the words* in the first verse will shift. Queens become Kings and 'her' becomes 'him'.

---

* FOOTNOTE: Only one other royal passing can beat this. When Elton John adapted his song 'Candle in the Wind' for the funeral of Diana Princess of Wales in 1997, 90 per cent of the lyrics to the first verse were changed.

The tune is not unique to Britain, either. The melody – if such it can be called – once backed the national anthem of Prussia, and Liechtenstein still employs it. When Northern Ireland played Lichtenstein in a qualifier for the Euro 96 football finals, the anthem was played twice. Iceland, Switzerland and Norway have their variations. The American patriotic song 'My Country, 'tis of Thee' is another example. The traditional tune was sung at the funeral of Senator John McCain in 2018, which must have raised some puzzled eyebrows among British viewers.

Oddly, for such an important song, there is no definitive version of 'God Save the Queen'. The number of verses and their content have changed with time and territory and context. Today, one verse is usual; occasionally two. The full six verses are rarely sung. The lyrics get increasingly goddy as the dirge progresses, and conclude with a line about crushing rebellious Scots – surely the world's only national anthem to press for a civil war.

Newspaper columnists are contractually obliged to question the national anthem once per year. Or so it seems. They argue that we should ditch 'God Save the Queen' and choose something else, a new national anthem either for England or for Britain as a whole. After all, the song does appear to be out of step with the shape of the nation, and not just because it calls for violence against rebellious Scots. Our national anthem is, in essence, an appeal to the almighty to look after the Queen (or King). Yet a 2017 poll by NatCen found that 53 per cent of British adults have no religious affiliation. We (and I am among them) must appeal to what we consider a fictional character if we want to display patriotism. Then we have the contingent who are proud of their country, but don't have much time for the monarchy. Britain's republican movement is small but not insignificant. Polls show that 15–20 per cent of the population would like to see the monarchy disappear up its own august fundament and give way to a republic. For roughly 10 million people, those 'long to reign over us' lyrics don't come easily. It's like making Luke Skywalker hum the Imperial March.

The trouble is, what do you replace it with? A common suggestion – occasionally used at sporting events – is 'Jerusalem', especially as an anthem specific to England. It has two downsides: it's a hymn, and so just as god-focused as the existing anthem; and it's named after a place that is not in England. 'Rule, Britannia!'* might fit the bill. It's certainly punchier than 'Jerusalem' or 'God Save the Queen', and contains only a speck of religious deference. It could serve well as an alternative British anthem, but not for England. 'Land of Hope and Glory' is another commonly cited contender. That, too, is a bit of a god-fest, but it also concerns itself with the onward expansion of the British Empire – a no-no in today's diverse society.

Nothing is quite appropriate. This is a good thing because it means that the perfect, custom-written song is yet to be penned. The opportunity is there for a budding composer to create something stirring but not jingoistic; a song that paints England as a bastion of freedom, tolerance and progress, without reference to supernatural beings, powerful overlords, conquering armies or the smashing of Scottish rebels. As we leave the European Union, the time is ripe for a fresh national anthem that reflects the society of today, not that of 200 years ago. If you have an ounce of musical talent, put this book down now and get on with it (I'd like a tenth of your royalties as my commission please).

---

* FOOTNOTE: Clock the punctuation, often erroneously left out.

Every British citizen has the right to vote

As we've seen elsewhere, senior royals are not barred by law from casting a vote. They choose not to do so by long-established custom, so as not to indicate a political leaning. That doesn't mean that everybody in the country has the right to vote. Far from it.

The first bunch of the disenfranchised is the largest, and most obvious. Extrapolating from 2011 census data, some 14 million people out of a population of 66 million are under 18. More than one-fifth of the population has no direct say in the democratic process.

The next largest group are convicted prisoners. Anyone serving time for a criminal offence is barred from the ballot. The UK prison population in 2018 stands at around 84,000. About 9,000 are foreign nationals, and so would be unable to vote in any case. That leaves around 75,000 people. A small fraction of these do, in fact, have a right to vote. These include unconvicted prisoners (those awaiting trial), or civil prisoners (those imprisoned for an offence that is not a crime, such as failing to pay child support). In addition, anyone found guilty of meddling with electoral practices is struck off the electoral register for five years.

Most foreign nationals living in the UK do not have the vote, but there are exceptions. Residents from Commonwealth countries can register if they have leave to stay. In addition, nationals from Ireland can also join the electoral register, thanks to the long-standing relationship between nations (Ireland was once part of the UK). No other EU countries have this privilege except for Cyprus and Malta, which are also Commonwealth nations.

Finally, those who sit on the red leather benches of the House of Lords must suffer a shortfall of suffrage. Members of that House – some 800 people – may vote in local elections, but they may not cast a vote in a General Election. The rationale is that members already sit in Parliament and can speak for themselves; they have no business electing somebody (an MP) to speak on their behalf.

Scottish banknotes are legal tender in England

Most banknotes circulating in England are printed by the Bank of England (at a plant in Wales, obviously). Most, but not all. Seven retail banks also have the right to print money: three in Scotland and four in Northern Ireland. When a Scottish banknote finds its way into English hands, mild panic often ensues. 'Argh, what's this? Is it legal tender? Will the shop accept it?'. The answers are 'A Scottish banknote', 'No' and 'Maybe'. But that needs a little unpacking.

Despite what friends might tell you, Scottish banknotes are *not* legal tender in England. But neither are they legal tender in Scotland (or anywhere). It's all down to a disconnect between the technical and popular definitions of 'legal tender'. In everyday parlance, 'legal tender' is any form of official cash. Strictly, though, it can only relate to the settlement of a debt, like a restaurant bill after you have eaten, or a bank loan. If you popped into a shop to buy this book, then legal tender doesn't enter into it. You simply swapped some cash (or electronic codes linked to cash) in exchange for this magnificent keepsake.

If you run up a bill in a restaurant, however, you are in debt to the business. You may pay for the meal with anything that is agreeable to the restaurant: coins, notes, cards, cheques (remember those?), magic beans, offers to do the washing up ... They may very well accept any of these. On the other hand, the restaurant is entitled to reject your chosen method. One still finds small cafés that won't accept cards, for example.

They *cannot* refuse legal tender or, to phrase it more accurately, they can't sue you for non-payment if you've offered to pay with legal tender. That means Bank of England notes and coins*.

Scottish banknotes are another matter. They do not qualify as legal tender in any circumstances or territory – even Scotland. Enjoy haggis in the Highlands or a wee dram in the Lowlands and no restaurateur would turn them down, but they could do if they wished. The banknotes hold the same status in England, but are more likely to be rejected due to unfamiliarity, ignorance or the universal nervousness that English people show towards Scottish money.

As mentioned above, day to day transactions – such as buying a pint of milk, or acquiring another of my books – are not subject to the rules of legal tender. A shopkeeper can refuse your cash, even if you offer Bank of England notes (try paying for chewing gum with a £50 note). Pleading 'But it's legal tender, you have to accept it' is simply not true on either clause.

The misconception was put to the test in 2016 in a most peculiar case. The Royal Mint occasionally issues commemorative £100 coins (yes, coins) for no apparent reason other than to spread delight among numismatists. One anonymous man bought 293 at face value, and no shipping fee, using his credit card. His ruse was to gain heaps of reward points on the card, then simply deposit the £29,300 of coins back into his bank account. The transactions would furnish him with enough air miles to pay for a round trip to Hong Kong – all at zero net cost. Can you see where this is going? (Hint: it's not Hong Kong.) The coins had been advertised as legal tender, but the man had misunderstood the term. He

---

* FOOTNOTE: It's actually a bit more complicated than this. Limits exist on smaller-denomination coins. Were you to rack up a £500 tab at The Ritz and attempt to pay for it in pennies, the management would be perfectly entitled to refuse your absurd purse. Pennies and two-pence pieces are only legal tender up to the value of 20p.

believed that his bank was obliged to accept the coins. They were not, and did not, and the man still has an unspendable heap of commemorative specie.

While we're talking cash, here's another little-known fact: the Queen's portrait is a relatively new feature on banknotes. The reigning monarch has always appeared on the coinage, but not on paper money. Her Majesty only gave permission for her likeness to appear on banknotes in 1961*, and initially only on the 10 shilling and £1 notes. Before the 1960s, Britannia was the presiding figure on all British notes. She's still there today, though relegated to a tiny roundel in the corner.

---

* FOOTNOTE: That's Bank of England notes. The Queen's portrait had appeared on many other currencies around the world. The first was a Canadian $20 banknote when she was just eight years old.

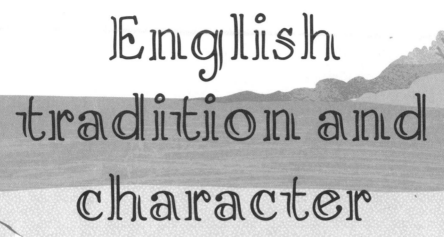

English tradition and character

We're on to the real stereotypes now, from drinking copious amounts of tea and warm beer, to an obsession with the weather.

CAFE

Punch and Judy is a fine old English tradition

The madcap puppet show has been a staple of outdoor entertainment for generations. If you've never had the pleasure, here's what you're missing. A puppeteer hides within a small booth, and performs his or her show through an opening in the top of the booth. Characters usually include a wonky-nosed buffoon (Mr Punch), his long-suffering wife Judy, a luckless child, Toby the dog, a crocodile, the occasional hangman, a policeman and a string of sausages.

The show is now aimed at kids but originally played as an adult satire. It is a *tour de force* of wife-beating, child abuse, cruelty to animals and inappropriate handling of raw meat. A 'fine old tradition' it ain't, though probably harmless even in these squeamish times. I think Charles Dickens's appraisal still holds: 'an outrageous joke which no one in existence would think of regarding as an incentive to any kind of action or as a model for any kind of conduct.'

Nor is it British. The Punch and Judy has its origins in 16th-century Italy. Punch was originally known as *Pulcinella*, which became *Punchinello*, thence Punch. The first record of a show in England comes from the pen of Samuel Pepys. In a diary entry for 9 May 1662 he records having observed an Italian marionette show in Covent Garden, London.

Punch and Judy has long-since lost its associations with Italy and is now considered a thoroughly British tradition (at least in this country). Variations can be found at the seaside, village fêtes and children's parties. It's rare to see the show in Covent Garden, though fans still gather on 9 May to celebrate Punch's 'birthday'. That's the way to do it.

'Ring-a-Roses' is a poem about the Great Plague

Ring-a-ring o' roses,
A pocket full of posies.
A-tishoo! A-tishoo!
We all fall down.

Like many a nursery rhyme, this familiar ditty has dark undertones. I can still remember the day, aged six or so, when I was told in school about the Black Death, and how the song I sang in the playground held a sinister echo of the plague.

It all checks out on face value. The 'ring-a-roses' represents the circular buboes that appeared on the skin of the afflicted. Those seeking to avoid the plague might carry a bunch of flowers ('A pocket full of posies') to ward off the bad aromas thought to cause the disease. The sneezing is self-evidently a symptom. And then we all fall down in death. Every line is easily mapped onto the horrific disease that killed half the population. Surely, this one is not a myth.

It seems so. No record of the song or dance can be found until 1855, when the *Brooklyn Eagle* refers to a hand holding game called Ring o' Roses. The lyrics were first printed in the 1860s and are very different to the modern words. No published version offers a sneeze until the 1880s, and then only in one of numerous variations. Most tellingly, nobody seems to have interpreted the song as a metaphor for plague until after the Second World War. The fact that the association appears to have started within living memory, means the idea that 'Ring-a-Roses' is an ancient plague song, all falls down.

It's always raining in England and this is all people talk about

I suppose, somewhere in a book about English character and misconception, I must to turn to the weather. The English really do like to talk about it. Our speech is soaked in meteorological idioms. As right as rain, fair-weather friend, under the weather, save it for a rainy day, you stole my thunder, come rain or shine, every cloud has a silver lining...

Place two random English people in a room together and there is a 50 per cent chance that the weather will be mentioned within the first minute. The only other outcome is that both remain mute. This is not, I would contend, because we are fixated with the forecast. It is the most pragmatic way to get a conversation going when you're a little bit awkward and know nothing about the other person. Everybody from millionaires to farmhands is affected by the weather. There are other universal topics that might be broached – What did you have for breakfast? How long since you went to the toilet? Do you like Donald Trump? – but those are too personal or confrontational. 'Fine morning today, eh?' is both general and harmless.

We have a lot of weather to talk about in the UK. As a nation made up of islands, we benefit from and bemoan the amount of moisture in the air. Our position close to the Gulf Stream can bring unseasonal warmth or cold. And yet England rarely suffers from extreme forms of weather that cause such a menace in many other countries. It is the unpredictability that is key. The rain shower from nowhere, or the sudden cold snap that leaves us regretting a lack of coat. This is all good fodder for the English habit of small talk.

The above notwithstanding, England's reputation as a damp and miserable country is exaggerated. Parts of the south-east went 50 days without a drop of rain in the summer of 2018. That was an unusual drought, but the norm is drier than many would suspect. Take London, for example. It is one of the driest capital cities in Europe. At 557mm (22in) (mean) of annual rainfall, it is notably less umbrella-worthy than Paris (631mm/25in), Dublin (758mm/30in), Rome (799mm/31½in) and the sodden city of Amsterdam (838mm/33in). Higher rainfall occurs elsewhere in the country, but it is no more prodigious than other comparable European nations. Pity Podgorica in Montenegro, which deals with some 1,661mm (65½in) per year.

Yes, it may rain on more days in England than elsewhere, if not with such vehemence. And, yes, those rains may come with less predictability. But England's changeable, middling but ultimately agreeable weather is the stuff that built our national character. I wouldn't want it any other way.

England is a nation of tea drinkers

One of the most reproduced images of wartime England shows a London housewife sipping a cup of tea upon the rubble of her former home. Everything she knows has been smashed by the Blitz. Her solace and refuge is a nice, warming cuppa.

The English do drink a lot of tea. This is true. It's been popular on these shores since its introduction in the mid-17th century. Over the generations, England has become intimately associated with the brown beverage. Browse any quarter-decent souvenir shop and you'll find teapots resembling Prince Charles, or loose leaves layered in a miniature red phone box. Taking afternoon tea at a posh hotel is a luxury treat for both tourists and locals alike. (Though it has to be said, the revived mania for high tea is as much down to Instagram as the product on offer.) And one might summon dozens of quotations from Great Britons, singing the praises of tea. I like this the best, from the 18th-century writer James Boswell:

'I am so fond of tea that I could write a whole dissertation on its virtues. It comforts and enlivens without the risks attendant on spirituous liquors. Gentle herb! Let the florid grape yield to thee. Thy soft influence is a more safe inspirer of social joy.'

We Brits, though, drink nowhere near as much tea as the record holders, the Turks. When assayed by the United Nations in 2016, the good people of Turkey got through 3.16kg (nearly 7lb) of tea per person per year. Second place went to Ireland with 2.19kg (4¾lb). The United Kingdom lags in third place with 1.94 kg (4¼lb). In other words, for every three cups of tea consumed in Britain, the Turks manage five.

As with scones (see page 95), the English delight in argument over how to make the perfect cuppa. One bloc holds that the milk should enter the cup first, with the brewed beverage poured on top. This is barbaric according to a counter-faction. One should pour the tea, and only then add the milk. To quote George Orwell, 'Indeed in every family in Britain there are probably two schools of thought on the subject.' All this presumes one is using a teapot. The vast majority of tea in England, I suspect, never sees the inside of a pot, and must suffer the indignity of mug-based infusion. Only 20 years ago, my grandmother was genuinely confused to see me bypass the teapot, as though the idea had never occurred to her. Today, it is surely the norm.

Tea, of course, has a second meaning in England. Those who live down south eat breakfast, lunch and dinner; those in the north do breakfast, dinner and tea. I grew up in a part of the Midlands where the latter taxonomy is ingrained. Even though I've now lived in London for two decades, I must still make a mental correction to say 'dinner' and not 'tea'.

The great evening meal divide can be mapped. A 2018 YouGov poll asked 42,000 people for their preferred terminology. The results show a clear switch in the Midlands above which no counties say 'dinner' and below which no counties say 'tea'. A minority of awkward types call it supper. The phenomenon seems to be independent of class. As to whether the midday meal should be lunch or dinner, the country is more divided. Children all over the nation get their school meals from dinner ladies, rarely lunch ladies. But as adults, southerners can say nothing but 'lunch'. It's all a bit of a dog's dinner, to be honest.

The English love warm, flat beer

I'm sat in a pub in Clapham. A very average pub in Clapham, though it is currently excelling itself by playing a mix of angsty jazz and forgotten 1980s classics. This is a pub very close to the train station, an undistinguished bar relying mostly on passing trade. Of its 25 taps 21 are from the keg (slightly fizzy, often cooled). That is to say, 84 per cent of its beer offerings don't fit the stereotype.

The idea that Brits drink warm, flat beer is as outdated as the cliché about us only drinking tea, or having no cuisine fit for consumption. The beer scene in England is world-leading, and getting better all the time. Almost every pub in the big cities now has a preponderance of choice, which includes traditional hand-drawn cask ales (the ones with big pump handles) alongside the more sparkling craft-keg beers (the ones with smaller taps). Both are typically drawn from the cellar, which will invariably be a few degrees lower than the place you're standing. If your ale is warm, then something has gone wrong.

How do you order a drink in a pub? To a Brit who boozes, the process is as instinctive as breathing. But visitors can find our system confusing and intimidating. Guide books don't normally cover this stuff because it seems so obvious, but it's my belief that everybody of drinking age should know how to procure a pint. This is how *not* to do it:

1. Enter pub.
2. Stand in doorway waiting to be seated.
3. Give up – the staff are no doubt busy – and find a seat for yourself.
4. Sit around trying to catch the eye of a member of staff.

5. Moan a bit about how this wouldn't happen in Berlin.
6. Approach the bar to complain.
7. Confuse the bartender by asking if someone can come and take the order.
8. Finally acquire drinks after a series of further misunderstandings.
9. Walk back to seat without paying, assuming it's all on a tab.

Hanging out in tourist centres like Covent Garden and Greenwich, I've seen all of these missteps on many occasions. For the record, this is the natural order of things:

1. Enter pub.
2. March up to bar like a champion.
3. Order your choice of drink.
4. Wait for the bartender to pour the drink.
5. Pay.
6. Take a seat.

It's that simple, and yet somewhat alien to many overseas visitors who are used to table service. Now, some British pubs will take orders at tables, but it's rare, and even these do most business at the bar itself.

Despite the stereotype that Brits love queueing, nobody has yet opened a bar with an organized queuing system. It just wouldn't be natural. Punters at a busy pub must instead squeeze into whatever gap presents itself and attempt to catch the bartender's eye. This is usually done by clutching a card or a tenner and placing that hand on the bar. Never wave it. Only practice and experience will allow you to effect the correct degree of assertiveness. One should be neither too strident, nor too limp-wristed.

It's common to be served out of turn. In such circumstances, the correct way to display annoyance is to gently grunt or sigh. You must hit a volume that is *just* audible to the person who got served in your place, but not so loud that they feel the need to react. The spurned customer, I've noted, will often swap their cash or card to the other hand, as though the wrong grip might have prejudiced the bartender's decision.

Overseas visitors might also be surprised at what's beneath their feet. Many traditional British pubs still clothe themselves in carpets, despite the frequent occurrence of tumbling liquids. You can often smell a well-doused pub carpet from the street – it's part of the charm. The ubiquitous JD Wetherspoon chain takes things to another level. All of its venues have individually designed carpets, with patterns that often reflect local history or landmarks. I've made it a life goal to photograph each one. I have no idea why, but a man's got to have a hobby. Cheers!

Everybody in England enjoys a good scone

Scones were invented to give English people an alternative subject for argument, when all aspects of the weather have already been considered. A scone is simply a thick, crumbly biscuit smeared in jam and cream. Little room for deviation is allowed. You can't, say, add a layer of chocolate or a flick of sprinkles and still call it a scone. That would be treason. It is surely because of this inflexibility that the scone is such a source of contretemps.

The first sticking point with the scone (assuming you've negotiated the jam) is how to pronounce it. Debating the alternatives is a national pastime. Should it be 'skone', to rhyme with phone, or 'skonn' to rhyme with 'John'? Southerners usually go with the former, while Northerners tend to favour the latter, but the rule is by no means universal and no doubt has an element of class preference. Someone has actually mapped the Great Scone Divide based on YouGov data. The 'John' scone is a clear winner north of a line that cuts through North Yorkshire, Lancashire and North Wales. But down in the South and the Midlands, we see a more equivocal situation. Much of these regions only report a 50–70 per cent favouritism for the 'phone' scone. We only see near-universality for this form in the London area, Essex and pockets of Derbyshire (perhaps centred on the Duke of Devonshire's excellent tea rooms). One form is no more 'right' than the other, of course, but that doesn't prevent the epic arguments every time the sweetmeat is presented. The only incorrect pronunciation is 'skoon', which is reserved for the Scottish village of Scone and its famous coronation stone.

Pronunciation is merely a sideshow for the big event. Every scone eater is aware that, before they can tuck into their treasure, they must perform the great gambit. Will they reach for the jam spoon or the cream spoon? The decision will reveal you as either a right-thinking person or a barbarous imbecile*. It depends on who is sitting opposite.

The front line of this battle is drawn between the neighbouring counties of Devon and Cornwall, traditional homes of the cream team. Devon proudly slops on the cream, then the jam, while Cornwall does the opposite. All over the country, dining partners bicker over which tradition to follow. In early 2018 a former royal chef revealed the Queen's own preference, and it is Cornish. If the highest exemplar of British tradition in the land dictates a jam-first approach (homemade Balmoral jam, no less), then the argument would seem to be settled. Unless you're a republican, in which case we're back to square one. Suggestion: can't we just whip the ingredients together into a pink fondue, and scoop this onto the scone?

Does every English man and woman crave a scone? It sometimes seems so. The elderly eat them with fondness and memories of the good old days. The young lap them up with a sense of knowing irony, and a mind for Instagram. Others indulge because they've been presented with a birthday 'tea and scone experience' at a posh hotel. Everybody eats them; everybody likes them.

Well not quite. I'm going to say something deeply offensive; a statement which I doubt has ever been made by an English writer in print before. It is simply this:

I do not like scones.

---

* FOOTNOTE: The dilemma is only rivalled by the great toilet-roll debate. Should you hang a roll so that fresh sheets are withdrawn from above or below? Twitter probably generates enough heated words on the topic each day to power its own servers.

I'm not vegan, and I do not have an intolerance to lactose. There is no financial or ethical barrier to me eating a scone. I am not watching my weight, and am happy to wolf down junk calories for the sake of a sugar rush. But I will not contemplate a scone.

I mean, what do people see in these things? The underlying biscuit-thing is drier than a mummy's palms. It's essentially dressed-up flour. Jam is fruit denuded of texture and cream is lard's fancier cousin. None of the three chief ingredients excites me and, when they come together, they are less than the sum of their parts. I get more delight from a single bourbon biscuit than I would from a plate of scones, no matter how you smother or pronounce them. I deride them, despise them, and fart in their general direction. Scone with the wind.

Sorry. I apologize that this section has slipped into a silly and subjective rant. But I feel this needs to be said. For too long a silent minority has held the scone in suspicion, baffled as to why anybody could prefer them over a flapjack or fudge cake. Yet we dare not speak out for fear of ridicule. That stops here. Let the rallying cry be heard throughout the land: it is OK to be English and not like scones.

Of course, if any reader would like to take me out to a posh hotel and buy me a luxury scone experience in a bid to convince me otherwise, then I am ever open to offers.

The English all eat huge fry-ups for breakfast

Eggs, bacon, beans, sausages, mushrooms, toast. This is the foundation upon which English greatness is built. The full English breakfast, listed on menus from the humblest greasy spoon to the poshest hotel, is deeply ingrained in the English way of life. I don't know anybody who eats them.

Not, at least, under normal circumstances. Who has time to fry up six or seven different ingredients first thing in the morning? Not anybody with a job or small children. And who, after decades of warnings about fat and cholesterol, would contemplate eggs, bacon and sausages every morning? According to a 2017 survey* around half the nation regularly skips breakfast entirely. I'm not sure if that figure rings true, but I am confident that only a small minority take time to cook anything more ambitious than toast. The full English is something we eat only in hotels, or perhaps as an occasional weekend treat if we want to impress the significant other.

Where does the English fry-up come from, and when was it invented? The greasy tableau we enjoy today has gradually evolved over time. In Victorian days, fried breakfasts were enjoyed exclusively by the wealthy. Only in the early 20th century did those on lower wages partake of bacon and eggs of a morning. By the 1950s, the traditional fry-up as we know it was largely in place.

---

* FOOTNOTE: Conducted by a porridge-oat manufacturer, and so should be taken with a pinch of salt, in both senses. The same survey found that 3 per cent of responders skipped breakfast because 'concerns about Brexit or the results of the US Election had curbed their appetite.'

England's glorious fauna and flora

With such a wide range of environments in a relatively small space, England is a superb country for wildlife lovers. You might be surprised to learn, though, just how many of our cherished plants and animals are immigrants.

Fallow deer: The fallow is perhaps the most familiar type of deer in Britain: a spotted, light brown body with a white underside. This is the species typically kept on private estates and large public parks. Wild populations are also widespread, particularly in the southern half of England. The deer were introduced by the Normans for hunting, although it seems that the Romans also brought over a small number. In fact, of the six deer species common in Britain, only two (the roe and the red) are truly indigenous. The most recent newcomer is the Reeves' muntjac, which escaped from private parks in the early 20th century and is now widespread.

Grey squirrel: This must be the most commonly sighted wild mammal in England. The blighters are everywhere. Head to a major park, and you may find one tame enough to climb up your leg, should you let it. Despite their ubiquity, grey squirrels only arrived in the UK from America in the early 20th century. The species has largely displaced the native red squirrel population, a cause of much teeth-gnashing among many Brits.

Horse chestnut: Pity the children of medieval England. Not only did they face a high risk of death from plague, typhoid, dysentery, smallpox and other diseases too numerous to mention, but they also couldn't play conkers. The horse-chestnut tree was not imported from Turkey until the time of Shakespeare. Other now-common trees from overseas include the copper beech, cypress, larch, London plane, plum and the ubiquitous sycamore. Even the English-to-the-core apple tree found its way here from central Asia at some distant date.

House mouse: The tiny, cute but deeply unpopular mammal has been with us throughout recorded history, but wouldn't have been familiar to earlier Britons. It arrived on our shores from continental Europe (and originally from Asia) sometime in the Iron Age, perhaps around 800BCE.

Parakeet: The flashy, green rose-ringed parakeet is now a common sight in south-east England – much to the surprise of anybody who visits from the north. Flourish an apple in Kensington Gardens and you'll be covered in the birds within seconds (a much-shared video of this happening to me can be found online). The birds are, of course, an invasive species, but are now the seventh commonest bird in the London region.

Pheasant: One often spies this colourful bird when driving through the countryside, though hopefully not on one's windscreen. The pheasant, native to Asia but treasured all over as a game bird, has graced the tables of nobility since at least the 11th century. The bird hunted by King Harold would have looked very different to that which we see today. Our present green-headed bird is thought to have been bred only in the 19th century, and its abundance in the countryside dates from a similar time.

Rabbit: *Watership Down, Peter Rabbit,* the trip down the rabbit-hole in *Alice's Adventures in Wonderland,* Wallace and Gromit's *Curse of the Were-Rabbit* … few creatures have made such a mark on English children's fiction. But the bunny ain't British. Rabbits were brought over by the Romans almost 2,000 years ago, though they do not seem to have established a wild population. Managed colonies were reintroduced in the 12th and 13th centuries but, again, the creatures did not live up to their modern reputation for fecundity. It is only since the 19th century that large populations of rabbits could be found in open countryside all over England.

Rats: England is home to two species of rat: the black and the brown. Neither is truly indigenous. Both originated in Asia, and made it to European ports as stowaways. The black rat got here first, not long after the Roman invasion. Later rattish immigrants brought in the two great plague epidemics in 1348 and 1665. The brown rat, by contrast, was not recorded in England until 1720. It has been highly successful, all but ousting the black rat in most parts of the country.

Stinging nettles: Would you whip yourself with nettles to warm up your body? Roman soldiers supposedly indulged in this pursuit, faced with the cold winters of northern England. They didn't use native plants, however. The stinging nettle we know and loathe today did not then grow in these isles. Our Roman overlords brought it over as seed, and cultivated the plant for food, remedies and a good thrashing. Next time someone waxes lyrical about 'What the Romans did for us', remind them of this unpleasant weed.

Historical bloopers

How many wives did Henry VIII actually have,
and should he be Henry IX?

King Harold, last of the Anglo-Saxon kings, was killed at Hastings

Every English school child learns the story of the Battle of Hastings. Brave King Harold, having put down a Danish invasion in the north, quick-marched down to the south coast to block the army of William of Normandy. Harold was mortally wounded by an arrow to the eye, during the decisive battle at Hastings. With Harold's death, Anglo-Saxon rule was over, and William was immediately crowned King of England.

Much of the above is untrue in some degree of detail. For starters, the great battle of 1066 – the most famous in English history – did not take place in Hastings. The site is almost certainly marked by Battle Abbey, some 9km (5½ miles) from the Hastings shore. William had the abbey built on the very spot where he vanquished the English king. This much is said in an obituary to King William, written just 20 years after the showdown.

The manner of Harold's death is also disputed. The arrow-in-the-eye story is not supported by contemporary accounts of the battle. Most descriptions lack detail, noting only that the king was slain. One exception is the so-called *Carmen de Hastingae Proelio*, probably written within a year of the battle. This poem vividly describes the death of the king, hacked to pieces with levels of gore that I refuse to quote in a family-friendly book. Suffice it to say that useful parts of Harold's body were relocated, and they did not include his eyes.

The first mention of death by arrow comes in a text 40 years after the battle – still within living memory, but open to inaccuracy. Other 12th-century accounts began to weave the detail in, and the tradition has been passed down the generations. The most powerful evidence, though, comes from the Bayeux Tapestry*. A famous image shows the figure of Harold grasping an arrow that is lodged in his face. The accompanying inscription tells us that 'Here King Harold is killed'. The chain of reasoning seems unassailable. It is not. First, the figure with the arrow might not be Harold. His name appears above, but elsewhere on the tapestry names and people do not always coincide. The king might equally be the woebegone figure to the right, stabbed and trampled by a Norman horse. Second, the arrow has been shown to be a 19th-century addition. Before this time, the figure held a spear shaft above his head. The arrow-in-the-eye story is perfectly possible, but what evidence we have for this incident is circumstantial at best.

History records that the short-lived reign of King Harold was immediately followed by his usurper, William of Normandy (or William the Conqueror, or William I, or William the Bastard if you must). It was a watershed moment in English history. The ancient House of Wessex was vanquished and with it the Anglo-Saxon era itself came to an end. The country would never be the same again.

Of course, nothing in human affairs is ever quite so clear cut. For the vast majority, toiling on farmsteads and wallowing in cow dung, life would carry on largely unchanged for generations. Sure, the local master might now flourish a French name and peculiar French habits. But the field still needed ploughing, the apples must be collected, and that pint of ale was not going to drink itself. The old way of life, the old language even, carried on without great change. Even the Anglo-Saxon Chronicles – an annual record of noteworthy events established by Alfred the Great – included

---

* FOOTNOTE: Which isn't, technically, a tapestry and wasn't made in Bayeux. See *Everything You Know About Art Is Wrong* for more discussion.

updates a century after the Conquest. We think of 1066 as a watershed retrospectively, and it certainly was in terms of distribution of power. For the common man and woman, though, it was business as usual. William's reign was, after all, the tenth the country had seen in just 52 years, including other invaders.

Nor did William automatically gain the crown upon slaying Harold. After Hastings, the surviving English bigwigs huddled together to elect a new king. That man was Edgar the Aetheling, grandson of King Edmund Ironside. Edgar, aged around 15, might have become the template for a thousand heroes of teen fiction, emerging as the unlikely young champion to rescue the kingdom from foreign invaders. It didn't quite work out like that. Edgar's advisors defected to William within weeks, and the Aetheling himself was bending a knee to the conqueror by the year's end. Surprisingly, he lived on into old age, a regular thorn in the side of the Normans, though nothing much more than a thorn.

Harold's burial site is also something of a mystery. If you were to visit Waltham Abbey in Essex (and you should, it has a first-class local museum), then you would encounter one contender. A lichen-encrusted stone in the former abbey grounds marks the supposed spot. Harold owned these lands and re-founded the church six years before his death. He stopped here to pray on his long march down to the battle near Hastings. References to his burial at Waltham Abbey begin not long after his death, but none quite convince. An alternative burial site in Bosham near Chichester has been suggested. Harold was born nearby, and an account written in the year of the battle suggests a coastal burial, but the facts are not conclusive. In the absence of evidence, numerous alternative theories have been offered, some even suggesting that Harold survived the battle and lived on in secret exile. It's tempting to conclude with a dismissive 'We shall probably never know' – but look what happened with Richard III.

The two-finger salute derives from the Battle of Agincourt

Agincourt is often cited as one of our greatest national victories – up there with Trafalgar, Waterloo, the Battle of Britain and the 1966 World Cup final. The battle took place south of Calais on 25 October 1415. The armies of England and Wales were numerically inferior to those of France, but they had a telling advantage: the longbow.

The French feared this long-range weapon. To deflect their jitters back onto the enemy, they threatened a ghastly mutilation. Any captured English archer would have his index and middle fingers severed. They would never fire a bow again. As it happened, the French cavalry was cut to pieces by arrows; they never got the chance to claim their digital bounty. The victorious English are said to have raised their bow fingers in a sardonic salute to the French – a gesture that is still common in the UK and some Commonwealth countries as a symbol of defiance.

It's a convenient if gruesome just-so story that has little basis in historical record. The usual punishment for captured soldiers was not mutilation but death (unless a ransom could be arranged, which was unlikely for archers, who were commoners). One source – a Burgundian writer present at the battle – does allude to finger slicing, but puts the threat in a speech by English king Henry V, whom he could never have heard. No accounts of the battle describe the English making two-fingered gestures at the cowed French. It might have happened but, like so much of medieval history, remains the stuff of rumour and hearsay rather than documented fact.

Tellingly, the myth was not written down before the 20th century. It is, most likely, a recent invention.

If that Agincourt connection does not seem daft enough, others have sought to stretch it to snapping point. The phrase 'pluck you', as a tempered version of the obscene phrase, has also been associated with Agincourt. The archers wielded bows made from yew, and so would pluck yew when firing at the French. The phrase 'flipping the bird', meaning to pull the one-finger salute – has also been linked to the battle. The bird is a reference to the feathers on the English arrows.

In truth, nobody knows where the two-fingered salute came from. Its first documented use dates only to the early 20th century. Quite possibly, it had been around for generations but was deemed too crude to be worthy of polite discussion in the printed record. It may have started as a variation on the middle-finger gesture, which was first recorded long before Agincourt in Ancient Greece.

Henry VIII had six wives

Go up to any person in the street and ask them to name one fact from English history. About 50 per cent of people will say that Henry VIII had six wives. (The other half will withdraw eye contact and speed off.) It's the ultimate everyone-knows-it fact. And it's wrong. On a technicality.

The portly monarch said his vows on six occasions, this much is true. His queens, as trivia fans can list, were Catherine of Aragon, Anne Boleyn, Jane Seymour, Anne of Cleves*, Catherine Howard and Catherine Parr. But here's the thing ... three of those marriages officially did not take place.

* FOOTNOTE: Despite her name, which has a hint of the executioner's block about it, Cleves was the longest-lived of all six wives. The divorcee outlasted her former husband by a decade.

Divorced, beheaded, died; divorced, beheaded, survived. So goes a popular mnemonic to remember the fates of Henry's wives. That word 'divorced' is not quite accurate, though. Henry's marriages to Aragon, Boleyn and Cleves were annulled, which is to say they were retrospectively declared invalid, as though the ceremony had never taken place. Legally, then, the corpulent monarch had only three wives.

Henry's multi-matrimonial conduct came entirely in his later years. His first marriage to Catherine of Aragon was surprisingly long-lived. The pair stuck together for 24 years. The mean length of time for a marriage that ends in divorce today is 11.7 years, so Henry was twice as steadfast as the modern standard. By contrast, his other five brides shared less than 10 years of matrimony. Anne of Cleves lasted just six months and three days beside the King though, uniquely, she remained friends with the monarch until his death.

Eight King Henrys have been crowned in England

Henry and Edward tie in first place as the most popular choice of name for an English (or British) monarch. We've had eight of each, ending with Henry VIII in 1547 and Edward VIII in 1936. But Team Henry has an ace up its sleeve, a secret, forgotten King Henry of the medieval period.

Henry the Young King (1155–83) was the second son of Henry II but became heir apparent on the death of his older brother in 1156. Unusually, young Henry was crowned as King of England while his father was still alive, a tradition popular in France. The ceremony took place in 1170, when Henry was still just 15. The boy had form as a precocious go-getter, having married a French princess when he was just five (and she was two). The pair carried the titles King and Queen of England for 13 years until Henry's death from dysentery in 1183.

All of this means that nine Henrys have been crowned in England though one, Henry the Young King, never reigned and so is not included in the chronology of monarchs.

Incidentally, were we to crown another King James, he would be styled as James VIII, even though England has never known James III–VII. Protocol now dictates that Scottish monarchs should be taken into account when assigning British regnal numbers. The last Jim-King was James II of England who was also James VII of Scotland. A future James isn't beyond the realms of the possible. At the time of writing, James Mountbatten-Windsor, eldest son of Prince Edward, is eleventh in the line of succession.

Walter Raleigh discovered tobacco

The Beatles don't have many forgettable songs in their oeuvre, but 'I'm So Tired' is arguably among them. Towards the end of that hymn to ennui, John Lennon curses Sir Walter Raleigh as a 'stupid get' for empowering his cigarette addiction. Raleigh might have been a stupid get in other ways – he did, after all, get himself executed – but it's a little unfair to blame a man dead for 350 years for your personal vices.

Raleigh, we're all taught at school, was responsible for introducing tobacco to England. Some accounts go further and suggest that he 'discovered' the weed in Virginia, or that he was the first to ship it to anywhere in Europe. None of these achievements could sit honestly on his CV.

In fact, it's doubtful that Raleigh ever set foot in Virginia, or anywhere else in North America. Between 1584 and 1589 he sent out expeditions to colonize the coast, and he named the region Virginia, perhaps in honour of the 'Virgin Queen' Elizabeth. But he did not personally superintend the missions. Virginian tobacco supposedly first reached England when a group of colonists returned in 1586. Raleigh soon got the court smoking, and the habit became fashionable. It was even touted as a cure for coughing.

The honeymoon didn't last long. In 1604, the newly installed King James I wrote *A Counterblaste to Tobacco*, in which he calls smoking 'A custom lothesome to the eye, hateful to the nose, harmful to the brain, dangerous to the lungs, and in the black and stinking fume thereof, nearest resembling the horrible stygian smoke of the pit that is bottomless.' He sounds like more of a vaping man.

Whatever Raleigh's influence in making tobacco fashionable, he was certainly not among the first huddle of English smokers. Close, you might say, but no cigar. The earliest Europeans to witness the habit sailed with Christopher Columbus in 1492. His scouts on the island of Cuba saw men inhaling smoke from charred sticks rammed with tobacco. Once its heady properties were fully appreciated, the plant soon made it back to Europe. The first tobacco merchant was recorded in Lisbon in 1533, more than half a century before Raleigh's courtly puffs. English sailors must have encountered it soon after. The slave trader John Hawkins brought his own stash of tobacco leaves back from the New World in 1565 and undoubtedly enjoyed a crafty smoke on English soil.

We English rally to Raleigh when asked about the history of tobacco, even though other Europeans got there decades before. The popularizer nearly always trumps the instigator. To end where we began, we might likewise praise The Beatles for giving the world 'Twist and Shout', even though the song had been recorded by two earlier groups.

Charles I was the last monarch to be put to death

Have you ever taken a selfie on Whitehall while standing beside the mounted soldiers? Check your photos, for they may have captured the mark of royal death. The clock of Horse Guards carries a black band beside the number two. It signifies the hour at which King Charles I was beheaded near this spot – at least if an old story is to be believed.

The execution of King Charles was a momentous event in English history. For the first time in 700 years, England had no monarch. This was the only period in which the country has functioned as a republic. The Interregnum was short-lived. Just 11 years separated Charles's execution and the Restoration that saw his son, Charles II, reclaim the throne. England (or Britain) never dabbled with republicanism again. We did, however, kill another king.

George V is today noted for three achievements. He was Queen Elizabeth II's granddad. He bestowed the word 'Regis' on Bognor Regis after reluctantly convalescing in the town. And he gave the country almost 500 playing fields by way of a memorial. He should also be remembered as the last British monarch to be murdered.

In 1928 the king fell ill with septicaemia and lung problems whose effects stayed with him for his remaining eight years. The following year, George spent 13 weeks in Bognor* under the slightly dubious but widely believed advice that seaside air is good for the constitution.

Finally, in January 1936, he could continue no longer and retired to his bedroom at Sandringham. After several days falling in and out of consciousness he passed away on 20 January.

George was not permitted a natural end. The king's physician Lord Dawson of Penn accelerated the inevitable by administering a lethal dose of morphine and cocaine. The ailing monarch was euthanized. These facts only emerged in 1986 with the publication of Dawson's private notes. The physician had taken the decision to end the king's suffering. Astonishingly, and by his own admission, Dawson gave the fatal injection before midnight so the news could break in the morning papers, rather than the 'inappropriate' evening news. Assisted dying was illegal in 1936. Dawson had effectively committed murder and, indeed, regicide. The establishment reacted by advancing him to Viscount a few months later.

The king's final words were either 'God damn you' or 'Bugger Bognor', depending on which story you believe. Either way, the campaign starts here to erect a clock at the West Sussex resort with a black mark beside the number 12.

---

* FOOTNOTE: Incidentally, his recuperation home was just 5km (3 miles) from the cottage where William Blake wrote of England's 'green and pleasant land' in his 1804 poem 'Jerusalem'; about 14.5km (9 miles) from Bosham, where we encountered Kings Harold and Cnut; and a similar distance from the site of England's oldest bones – those of 'Boxgrove Man' dating back half a million years. West Sussex really is an under-appreciated nexus of English myth and history.

All British women got the vote in 1918

I'm writing this section on 6 February 2018, precisely 100 years since the Representation of the People Act was passed. In other words, it's a century since British women got the vote. The anniversary has rightly prompted much celebration and commemoration. A statue of suffragist Millicent Fawcett now stands in Parliament Square; special coins were minted; exhibitions and events were held up and down the land. Yet that landmark legislation did not go as far as simple 'women got the vote' statements would suggest. Millions of women were still disenfranchised.

To be eligible to vote, a woman had to be at least 30 years old. For men, the minimum age was 21. The rationale was sexist. So many men had been killed in the First World War that women now made up a clear majority of the population. For every 100 men, there were 110 women. Had the sexes been granted age parity, then women would have made up a majority of the electorate, an unpalatable outcome for the establishment of the time*. Women also had to meet certain property requirements. This was minimal – they had to inhabit a property with a rateable value greater than £5, which most women did – but it counted as a limitation that no longer held back men.

It's often forgotten, but the Act also enfranchised plenty of men who had hitherto sloped impotently past the polling station. Before 1918, about one-third of the male population was disenfranchised because they failed

---

* FOOTNOTE: That said, the same Act gave women as young as 21 the vote in local elections, the same as men.

to meet the property requirements. Basically, they were too working class. With the 1918 Act, more than five million men gained the vote alongside more than eight million women. The overall electorate trebled.

A further Act of 1918 allowed women to stand for parliament. The first lady to be elected was Constance Markievicz in the General Election of that same year but, as a member of Sinn Féin and as a resident of Holloway Prison, she stayed clear of Westminster. It was not until December 1919 that the back benches of the House of Commons felt the brush of skirts, when Nancy Astor became the first female to sit in the House. Finally, in 1928, a further Act gave women the vote from age 21, with no property restrictions. In 10 years, Britain had gone from being a country where no women could vote to one in which the majority of the electorate was female.

Let's finish with a little-known chapter from half a century before the Representation of the People Act. To say that (some) women first got the vote in 1918 is not strictly true. An 1867 by-election in Manchester granted the right to vote to all ratepayers, but neglected to specify the men-only rule. Scottish shopkeeper and widow Lily Maxwell was one such ratepayer and found that her name had been included on the electoral register. At the polling station, the clerk had 'no alternative but to take the proffered vote and record it along with those tendered by persons of the more favoured sex.'

The loophole was soon closed, preventing further outrages against democracy, but not before Maxwell's actions had sparked heated debate. We leave the topic with a verse of praise for the forgotten Maxwell, who eventually died penniless in a workhouse. It is taken from the pages of *Punch* magazine, and offers sartorial suggestions for future suffragists:

And when in the course of the ages,
Which in good time all good measures bring,
Our *femmes soles*, like birds out of cages
Released, on the register sing,
To the poll, as on steel-stiffened pinions,
Once doves, henceforth eagles, they press,
Let a bright Lily badge deck the chignons,
And be clan-Maxwell tartan their dress.

England has not been invaded since 1066

Large construction sites sometimes hang up notices declaring, say, '262 days since last accident'. The British psyche does something similar. As an island nation, we're tricky to invade. Most regions of continental Europe have been conquered, lost, reconquered and fallen again, many times over. Not so Blighty. We can look back at almost a thousand years of stability, without interference from hostile countries. The Norman invasion of 1066 represents the last time England was taken by a foreign power.

Well, you know by now how this book works, so you'll already have sensed that I'm building up a straw man. Depending on how you define 'invasion' and 'successful', the country has been successfully invaded on numerous occasions. The Scottish, for example, made regular incursions over the border in the later Medieval period, sometimes occupying English lands for many years. Nothing since 1066 could rightly be described as a 'conquest', but at least three incidents led directly to regime change in England.

French occupation: England occupied by French soldiers for 16 months? It happened. The First Barons' War is the term given to the little-known events that followed the 'signing' of Magna Carta. That document theoretically reduced the power of King John and give more say to the barons, a wealthy landowning elite. John didn't play ball, and the barons returned to a state of indignance that brewed into civil war. Then the French got involved. Prince Louis, heir apparent to the French throne, sided with the barons and sent over an invasion force. It landed in Kent in May 1216 and made swift progress. London was taken without a fight – its citizens were sympathetic to the cause – followed by much of southern England. Louis was even proclaimed (though not crowned) king in a ceremony at St Paul's Cathedral. Many battles and sieges followed before the death of John in October 1216 removed the key antagonist. The French lingered for another year, still in control of much of England. A series of defeats and baronial defections to the new King Henry III finally forced Louis and his men out of the kingdom.

Invaders force king's abdication: The year 1326 saw another partly successful invasion that shook up the status quo. Isabella, Queen of England, had fallen badly out of favour with her husband Edward II (he of red-hot poker fame), and madly in love with the exiled nobleman Roger Mortimer. The two drew together a small army of continental mercenaries, backed by troops from the Lowlands, and sailed across the channel to Suffolk. Edward's regime was unpopular, and many lords flocked to Isabella and Mortimer. As the invasion gathered momentum, royal power crumbled and the king was forced to abdicate in favour of the young Edward III. The episode was essentially the culmination of a civil war, but it was undeniably brought about by a foreign invasion force headed by Isabella, daughter of the French king.

Another king toppled by a Dutch invasion: Perhaps the best known invasion of England was also the most peaceful. In 1688, the unpopular James II (James VII of Scotland) was hounded out of the country by a Dutch invasion force led by William of Orange. William was Protestant and had the blessing of many among the English ruling class who despised the incumbent king's Catholicism. The Dutch army and navy met little resistance, and William soon took the Crown jointly with his wife (and James's daughter), Mary. The 'Glorious Revolution', as it was swiftly dubbed, marks the last time that England was successfully invaded, albeit by invitation.

The great misunderstood characters of England

From the warrior queen to the king of cigars, England's roll call of heroes and villains is replete with misconceptions.

Queen Boudicca or Boudica or Boadicea or Boudicea

Westminster Bridge is home to an astonishing sculpture. Stand beneath Big Ben and look north. Two rampant horses draw a chariot of war, its wheels nastified with fearsome spikes. The chariot carries a queen and her half-naked daughters, hellbent on a mission of revenge. It is a symbol of rebellion, uprising and anger at authority. How very British to place such a symbol next to the seat of national government.

A plaque beneath the statue tells us that this is 'Boadicea, Queen of the Iceni, who died AD61 after leading her people against the Roman invaders'. Boadicea is one of the first women of Britain whose name is recorded. Ironic then, that the name has been incorrectly recalled for generations. Boadicea is better written as Boudicca, for reasons that shall become clear.

We know so little about the lady. Only two ancient accounts of her reign survive, those of the Romans Tacitus and Cassius Dio. Both are written after the events (in Cassius Dio's case, more than a century had elapsed) and both vary in their detail. The basic story, as far as known, is this. Boudicca was Queen of the Iceni tribe, based in present-day Norfolk, at the time of the Roman invasion. The two powers got along peacefully for a couple of decades, and the Iceni were left to get on with their own affairs without interference. It couldn't last, and soon the Romans were edging into Iceni territory. Soon it was all out war. Boudicca's daughters were captured and raped and the queen was subjected to a flogging. She vowed revenge and brought sword and fire upon the Roman towns at Colchester, London and

St Albans. An estimated 70,000 died in the conflict and the cities were razed to the ground. Boudicca was eventually defeated by the Romans, at a battle site whose location is still mysterious. She remains a symbol of British resistance.

When dealing with such poorly documented events, it is difficult to say what is truth and what is myth or exaggeration. But we do know that the queen was not known as Boadicea. For generations, school children were taught that name. Then, rather recently, it switched to Boudica or Boudicca. It's hard to let go of a truth that's hard-wired from school days, and many still cling to the name Boadicea like stubborn charioteers. The spelling is reinforced beneath that statue on Westminster Bridge.

Yet the original sources call her Boudicca (not just in translation, but also in the original Latin). The spellings Boadicea and Boadicia were introduced in Tudor times, then popularized by 18th-century poet William Cowper in his 'Boadicea, an Ode'. This appellation became standard until recent times,

when scholars and teachers returned to the original sources. *The Telegraph* newspaper, ever the bastion of conservative values, still dictates 'Boadicea, not Boudicca' in its style guide.

Many gaps remain in the story of Boudicca, and they have been filled by speculation and nonsense. Her burial site is a case in point. It has never been found. A spurious tale places her final resting place beneath platform 9 or 10 of King's Cross Station – the same spot where J.K. Rowling has the Hogwarts Express departing with Harry Potter and friends. The legend partly derives from the ancient name of King's Cross, which is Battle Bridge. Etymologists think the term came from much-bemangling of the name 'broad-ford' bridge, denoting a crossing built over the River Fleet hereabouts. No evidence of an actual battle has ever been uncovered in King's Cross, unless you count the frequent bun fights to get served at a local burger restaurant, which my editor won't allow me to name.

Lady Godiva, naked equestrian

Like Boudicca, Lady Godiva was also an historically documented figure who is now shrouded in mythology. Godiva, or Godgifu was the wife of Leofric, Earl of Mercia, and died at some point soon after the Norman Conquest. The pair were well known in their day for their generous donations to monasteries. All these good deeds would be eclipsed in memory by one single act by Godiva: a naked ride through Coventry.

It all began, improbably, with a tax dispute. Leofric, for reasons lost to history, had imposed punishing taxes on the people of Coventry. Godiva pleaded time and again with her husband, begging him to reduce the burden. He refused but, in jest, offered to lower the taxes if his wife would ride through the streets of Coventry naked. The countess found a way to call his in-the-buff bluff. She ordered the town to remain indoors with their windows boarded while she partook of canter immodest. Just one person broke ranks. A tailor called Thomas peered out of his window to watch the disrobed noble. This is the origin of the phrase 'peeping Tom'.

It's a powerful story: self-sacrifice for a noble cause, with more than a hint of titillation. But the episode is not recorded in any chronicle of the time. That's unsurprising. Leofric controlled the local scribes. He could easily have redacted the embarrassing incident from the official record. It is not mentioned in written document until the *Flores Historiarum* manuscript of 1265 – more than 200 years after the supposed nude procession. Who knows what truth was left in the story after two centuries of Warwickshire whispers. In that account, Godiva rode through the market to a full audience, and there is no mention of a peeping Tom. Which goes to show how myths accrete new details with time.

St George was a proper English hero

'Cry "God for Harry, England, and Saint George!"' So implores Henry V at Harfleur, the line that ends Shakespeare's famous 'Once more unto the breach, dear friends' speech. This Saint George fellow has long served as a talisman for the English, from the battlefield to the football terraces. Yet the national saint was not of the nation.

The historical George – if he existed at all, for the sources verge on the mythical – never so much as heard of England. He couldn't have done. He was martyred around 303CE, when the country that would one day venerate him was still known as Britannia. It would be more than a century before the Angles, after whom England is named, bothered these shores.

Nor did he visit. According to the legends, George was a Roman soldier of Greek or Turkish (to use the modern term) descent, who was tortured and executed after refusing to give up the Christian faith. Very few particulars of his life are known, but no hint suggests that he ever travelled west of Greece. The dragon-slaying story, it hardly needs stating, is entirely made up. The earliest sources about his life (4th or 5th century) don't feel the need to describe George's run-in with a fire-breathing monster, and this is only recorded from the 11th century. By one tradition, the encounter took place on a hill at Uffington, a little east of Swindon.

How, then, did this east European of sketchy biography become the patron saint of England? The answer is, gradually. For much of the later medieval period, Edward the Confessor was regarded as the country's most important saint. George's star began to rise when crusading knights brought home tales of his exploits from the Byzantine Empire. A century later, Edward III chose the dragon-slayer as the patron saint of the Order of the Garter, the most prestigious mark of chivalry a knight could attain. George's story was spread far and wide by the coming of the printing press, and he soon gained veneration as the national protector.

The English are not the only ones to march behind his shield. As its name hints, the nation of Georgia also counts our man as its patron saint. The national flag is a St George Cross with four miniature red crosses in the quadrants. You'll also see the familiar red and white on the flag of Barcelona. George is also venerated throughout other parts of the Iberian Peninsula. In fact, he pops up everywhere – from the flag of Moscow to the Brazilian football team Corinthians, who formerly played at the Estádio Parque São Jorge, and sometimes wear an emblem of St George on their kits.

St George's Day in England, 23 April, is a muted affair compared with the revelry that surrounds the Irish celebration of St Patrick, but that perhaps is changing. The date has resonance throughout English history. The reign of England's greatest king, Alfred, began on 23 April 871. It is the traditional birthday of William Shakespeare and the date of his death. Namesake George V, who I'm beginning to think is the patron monarch of this book, also pulled a biggy on 23 April. On this date in 1924, the monarch made the first royal broadcast, while opening the British Empire Exhibition at Wembley. And, no, he didn't say 'Bugger Bognor'.

King Arthur, once and future king of England

King Arthur isn't simply one of the most famous kings in the history of England, he's the *only* famous Brit between Boudicca and Alfred – a span of some 800 years. Sure, some people will be able to name King Offa whose dyke we met earlier. Quite a few will be aware of St Augustine, who returned Christianity to the country in the 6th century – but he was from Italy. The Venerable Bede is familiar to anyone who spends time reading about the period, but is hardly a household name. King Arthur is the only British personality to shine out of the dark ages into the popular imagination. That he never existed is quite probable.

Arthur's legend comes to us in fragments, accreted over centuries into a tale that is much embellished from its earliest forms. Most accounts place the hero in the late 5th or early 6th century. This was a hundred years after the Roman legions had departed Britain, when the island was under invasion from Germanic tribes we now know as the Angles and Saxons. Arthur stood, so the legends say, as a beacon of noble Romano-British resistance in the face of the aggressors.

The earliest references to King Arthur come in a 9th-century manuscript, written 300 years after the supposed events it details. The *Historia Brittonum* provides us with a tasty list of the king's great battles. That Arthur supposedly slayed 960 men *single-handedly* at the Battle of Badon tells you everything you need to know about the manuscript's relationship with reality. No primary evidence from the time of Arthur's putative reign exists, and the other early accounts come centuries later and are dubious. It is possible that an historical Arthur existed, but the sober historian can offer nothing of substance to prove it.

Arthurian legend as we know it was largely woven by Geoffrey of Monmouth in his 12th-century *Historia Regum Britanniae*. It's worth highlighting the distance here. Geoffrey was writing 600 years after the death of Arthur (if he ever existed). That's akin to me penning a history of the Battle of Agincourt without access to the Internet, decent libraries or to any modern scholarship. Basically, I'm going to make stuff up to fill the inevitable gaps and, while I'm at it, I might as well add a bit of spice. Geoffrey did just that, and it's impossible to separate his ripping yarns from any genuine historical detail he might have gleaned from now-lost manuscripts.

Geoffrey's writings tell us little of historical worth, but are of enormous cultural importance – setting the scene not just for Arthurian legend but also the story of King Lear and the mythical founding of London by Brutus. Not bad for a single work. The cleric's pen gave us the first taste of the wizard Merlin and Arthur's bride Guinevere. Arthur's father Uther Pendragon and the sword Excalibur are also first namechecked by Geoffrey. All of these pivotal characters came hundreds of years after the earliest sources about Arthur and are more likely Geoffrey's invention than historical characters. The much-celebrated Round Table and the Sword in the Stone are still later innovations. That the Knights of the Round Table dance whenever they're able and impersonate Clark Gable is thought to be a 20th-century amendment.

Arthur's sword is often a source of confusion. Everybody knows the king wielded a mighty blade called Excalibur. And everybody also knows that he drew the sword from a stone, thus proving his worth as king. Historic legends of Arthur usually imply that these are separate swords. Arthur gains Excalibur from the Lady of the Lake, to whom it is returned upon his death, whereas the Sword in the Stone is unnamed. The two are often conflated because, well, it makes a tidier story.

King Alfred, the burner of cakes

After Arthur (whose existence is dubious), King Alfred is the most famous figure from the long, poorly chronicled centuries between the Romans and the Normans. He is known to posterity as Alfred the Great. And rightly so. This was a man skilled with both pen and sword; a scholar-king who could batter Vikings while dreaming about libraries.

Alfred* became King of Wessex in the year 871. It was a turbulent time to take on the Crown. Danish invaders were ingurgitating England like mead. Swathes of the country were under Viking control. In his first year as king, Alfred fought nine bloody battles with the invaders in a desperate bid to hold on to his inheritance. By 878, all the Anglo-Saxon kingdoms bar Wessex had fallen to the Danes, and Alfred was under the cosh. At one juncture, the great man was forced into hiding in the marshes of Somerset to preside over a sodden realm of puddles and moorhens. Things were not looking good.

This low point in Alfred's career was also the wellspring of his most enduring biographic detail. According to folklore, the incognito ruler was asked to keep an eye on a batch of cakes by a local peasant woman. The distracted king, pondering his comeback, allowed them to burn. He was promptly scolded by the peasant, who was unaware of his identity.

---

* FOOTNOTE: More properly Ælfred, and pronounced at the time something like 'A-eel-fred'.

It's not the most sparkling anecdote, is it? A minor domestic accident that happened in a swamp 1150 years ago. Arthurian capers aside, Alfred's charred buns are the most commonly recalled event in British history from before the Norman Conquest. Thousands of years of Neolithic, Celtic, Roman and Anglo-Saxon comings and goings and all anyone remembers are some charred baps. We Brits love to mock those in positions of power. Incidents like this remind us that even the great and the good are prone to bouts of doltishness.

But did 'Cakegate' ever happen? Nobody knows. No written record of the incident exists until three centuries after it supposedly happened. It's perfectly possible, but undocumented. A similar, and earlier, tale is told about the ludicrously named Danish invader Ragnar Hairybreeks – perhaps this man's culinary accident was borrowed by Alfred's biographers.

Whether there is a crumb of truth in the story may never be known, but Alfred's true legacy is more certain. The king went on to defeat and settle with the Vikings. More than this, he introduced programmes of literacy and legislation that changed the direction of the nation. Alfred, though, could not claim to be king of all England as is often written. Only in 927, when Athelstan seized the north of the country from the Danes and declared himself King of the English, was the whole land united under one ruler. Indeed, Athelstan also received the submission of Constantine II, King of the Scots, and so effectively became King of the whole of Britain (a title he had stamped on coins). This he achieved some 660 years before the Kingdoms of England and Scotland were united under the personal rule of James I and VI.

Robin Hood and his merry men

As with King Arthur, Robin Hood is a character of myth who may have had some basis in reality, though the evidence of his career is thin. It would be incorrect to say that no records survive to support his existence. Actually, the opposite is true. The medieval bandit's calling card crops up time and again in ancient records. Robin and Robert were common names. Hood, too, was also reasonably widespread. One theory suggests 'Robin Hood' was a generic name for any outlaw, much as today we use Joe Bloggs, John Doe and Alan Smithee to represent an everyman, an unidentified corpse and a disgruntled film director, respectively. We will probably never know if there was a single individual who gave rise to the Robin Hood myth, or whether he was assembled from the adventures of several unrelated bandits. We *do* know that many of the key elements of Robin's story were invented hundreds of years after he supposedly lived.

Today, the Hoodster is usually painted as a nobleman gone feral; a robber-baron turned robber of barons. A prince of thieves. Yet the earliest references to Robin Hood (13th and 14th century) all place him in the yeoman class – the sort of fellow who might hold a little farmland or look after a household. If he had any connection to noble blood at all, it would be have been via the handle of a mop after a jousting tournament. The tradition of the fugitive lord came from the time of Shakespeare when, in 1601, playwright Anthony Munday elevated Robin to the Earldom of Huntingdon. The association seems to have stuck. The current, real-life Earl of Huntingdon is named William Edward Robin Hood Hastings-Bass.

The modern story almost always frames Robin as a champion of Richard the Lionheart – the great English crusader king*. In the boo-hiss corner is John, corrupt caretaker during his brother's absence in the Holy Land. The timing is plausible. Richard reigned in the last decade of the 12th century, about 80 years before Robin's first mention in historic records. Yet it is not until the Tudor era, some 300 years after the Lionheart's death, that the outlaw appears on the same pages as the crusading king and his maligned brother.

Did he rob from the rich to give to the poor? The earlier accounts don't suggest so. His wealth-redistributing habits are again first mentioned in Tudor times. Specifically, historian John Major is the first to make the association, writing in 1521 that Robin '... permitted no harm to women, nor seized the goods of the poor, but helped them generously with what he took from abbots.' Of course, his antihero actions might have been celebrated in song or oral tradition that has not been recorded, but no earlier ballad or text confirms this.

Many of the well-known characters are also later inventions. Little John was there from the beginning, although the famous scene of Robin and John battling with quarterstaffs on a bridge is a 17th-century invention. Maid Marian was fashionably late to the party. A similar character of that name crops up in other medieval traditions, but only crossed over into the Robin Hood universe (to use the terminology of the Netflix generation) during the 16th century. Friar Tuck seems to have had a similar genesis, transitioning from a common figure of fun at May festivals, to a proper Merry Man in the 15th century. Alan-a-Dale had to wait until the 17th century.

Each generation adds to the myth. We're still at it. In the 1970s, Walt Disney portrayed the bandit as a fox, with Little John a bear. The 1980s film *Time Bandits* painted Robin as an upper-class twit. The 1991 Kevin Costner adaptation added Azeem, a Moorish character played by Morgan Freeman, to the band of outlaws. Around the same time, starship captain Jean-Luc Picard found himself transformed into the outlaw by an omnipotent alien, complete with an android Friar Tuck and a Klingon Will Scarlet.

---

* FOOTNOTE: Who, incidentally, may have spent as little as six months of his reign in England.

Other modern retellings have posed the comrades as children, Muppets, Smurfs, robots and anime characters. The point is that the Robin Hood legend is protean, adapted to the times. It began life as a fireside story, shaped by the whims of the storyteller. Modern twists to the tale might seem inauthentic or even ridiculous, but they are all in a centuries-long tradition of Hood-winking. And *that* is why I asked my illustrator to depict Robin Hood on a pogo stick.

Dick Turpin, dashing thug

The quintessential highwayman was a real figure, but our modern impression of him as a dashing, romantic character is more myth than reality. Turpin was probably a thuggish, unattractive man. No contemporary drawings exist, but a few descriptions were made in the newspapers. One 1737 account marks the man as 'about five Feet nine Inches high, of a brown Complexion, very much marked with the Small-Pox, his Cheek Bones broad, his Face thinner towards the Bottom, his Visage short, pretty upright, and broad about the Shoulders.' He murdered on at least one occasion and was implicated in many savage beatings. Far from the gentlemanly desperado of legend, Turpin was a pock-marked delinquent.

The Turpin fairytale was largely the creation of William Harrison Ainsworth. His novel *Rookwood* (1834) was published almost a century after the outlaw's execution, and takes many liberties with reality. Turpin is only a secondary character in the story, but nevertheless looms large and glamorous. His frenetic ride to York is particularly well-realized. Trusty mare Black Bess accomplishes the 200-mile flight in less than a day (the stagecoach took four), before dying of exhaustion at the edge of that city. 'Gone, gone! and I have killed the best steed that was ever crossed! And for what?', cries Dick.

For a great deal, as it happens. The fictitious ride to York cemented the Turpin legend in the popular imagination. He is now so established as an archetype that few people could name any other highwayman. The truth is very different. Turpin operated as a highway robber for just four years, following a longer career as a poacher, house breaker and thief (notably stealing horses and deer). Even then, press reports unequivocally linking him to highway hold-ups are scarce, and he was eventually convicted for horse theft.

Black Bess is a figment. As a horse thief, Turpin took many steeds for a test drive, yet there is no record that he ever favoured one particular mare. The name Black Bess is probably a 19th-century invention, taking hold in pamphlets and other ephemera before establishing its place in the Turpin canon through *Rookwood*. No horse can travel 200 miles in one day under its own power.

Winston Churchill's bon mots

Question: Who said 'We shall fight them on the beaches'?
Answer: Nobody. In his famous oratory, Winston Churchill actually said 'We shall fight on the beaches ...'. He didn't specify a 'them', at least not in that part of the speech. Germans, Italians, starfish, each other ... he could have meant anything. That's why Churchill is nearly always misquoted as saying 'fight *them* on the beaches', which I suppose still isn't 100 per cent clear, but at least rules out the 'each other'.

Churchill, more than any English figure of the 20th century, is mythologized, misquoted, misunderstood and, in some quarters, missed. Whole books have been written about 'the real Churchill', implying that it is a 'fake Churchill' who stalks the popular imagination. The misquote above is but a grain of sand on a landing beach of misinformation. Did Churchill let Coventry burn to protect the secret intelligence gathered by British codebreakers? Did he know in advance about the attack on Pearl Harbor, but withhold information to draw America into the war? Was the bombing of Dresden really a direct reprisal for Coventry, or a strategic mission to help the Red Army? These weighty questions are better left to military historians, and I'd guide you to the excellent International Churchill Society website winstonchurchill.org for detailed discussion and source material. Still, there's much about Winnie's character and reputation that is more readily tackled.

Let's start with his rousing speeches. Did Churchill even give them? That seems like the stuff of conspiracy theories, but the notion has been given serious examination. Rumour has long persisted that an exhausted Churchill handed over some of the greatest oratory in human history to an impersonator. The nation was hoodwinked into believing the Prime Minister was addressing them directly over the radio. Churchill certainly delivered his most famous speeches on their first reading in the House of Commons. This was long before recording equipment was present in the House, so the only ears to hear those rousing words were the assembled Members and those in the press gallery. The 'We will fight on the beaches' speech of 4 June 1940 was particularly well received. The Prime Minister had turned the fall of France and the evacuation of Dunkirk into a statement of defiance and the beginnings of national victory. 'Several Labour members cried,' noted one MP.

How his words reached the wider nation is another story. The speech was never read in its entirety over the radio, though news reporters repeated the key phrases. According to orthodox history Churchill did not record the speech until 1949, and it is this recording that has sent shivers down British spines ever since. The power and confidence in those words was such that many people recalled hearing the Churchillian delivery long before 1949. Step onto the scene Norman Shelley.

Shelley was an actor noted for roles on *BBC Children's Hour*. He also fancied himself as a bit of a Churchill impersonator and claimed to have acted as such in an official capacity during the war. Recordings of Shelley reading Churchill's key speeches are known, though there is little evidence they were ever broadcast. The story resurfaces from time to time as new evidence emerges, but no one has yet definitively shown that the Prime Minister used a stand-in.

In this case, it seems Churchill really did say what people remember him saying, but he's also attributed with numerous quotes he never uttered:

- 'The best argument against democracy is a five-minute conversation with the average voter.'
- 'You have enemies? Good. That means you've stood up for something, sometime in your life.'
- 'If you're going through hell, keep going.'
- 'If a man is not liberal in youth he has no heart. If he is not conservative when older he has no brain.'
- Of Clement Attlee: 'He is a sheep in sheep's clothing!'. This may have been spoken by Churchill, but the incident is unverified.

Did you know that Winston Churchill was saved twice by the same man? As a youngster, Winston was swimming in a Scottish lake when he encountered difficulties. The flailing lad was pulled to safety by a farm boy named Alex. In gratitude, Winston's family paid for Alex to attend medical school. Alex, full name Alexander Fleming, would go on to discover penicillin. This antibiotic later saved Churchill's life when the Prime Minister fell ill during the height of the Second World War. Without Churchill we wouldn't have had Fleming, and without Fleming we wouldn't have had the key years of Churchill.

It's a lovely, circular story but, sadly, hardly a word of it is true. Fleming was born into a Scottish farming family, but no records place the Churchills in the region during his childhood. Nobody has ever found evidence that the Churchills paid for Fleming's education, nor that Churchill ever took penicillin. Though he did suffer infections during the war, they were treated with a different class of drug by a different doctor.

We finish on a petulant, pedantic note. Churchill is a figurehead of Allied victory in the Second World War, but he no longer held power when that war finally ended. The General Election of 1945 brought Labour into power under Clement Attlee. Although Churchill witnessed the fall of the Nazis as Prime Minister, and declared victory in Europe, the war continued in the Far East. It was Attlee who occupied 10 Downing Street when Japan surrendered, signalling the end of the Second World War.

And the rest
of the Kingdom

Although we've focused on England, the UK contains three other countries: Northern Ireland, Scotland and Wales. Is everything we know about these nations wrong as well?

Auld Lang Syne: The phrase is often attributed to the poet Robert Burns, who wrote the well-known poem-song of the same name in 1788. He borrowed it. A poem from the beginning of the 18th century by Sir Robert Ayton is the first documented use of the term, written as 'old long syne'. That same poem also opens with the words 'Should auld acquaintance be forgot' and, indeed, the acquaintance has been forgotten in favour of Burns.

Bagpipes: There are two types of people in this world: those who despise the sound of bagpipes, and those who play them. Cheap joke. I'm sorry. But it has to be acknowledged that the droning instrument is not universally popular. The pipes are intimately associated with the Highlands of Scotland, yet the instrument has origins in the ancient world. The Roman emperor Nero, more usually and apocryphally associated with fiddling while Rome burned, was an early pioneer. Bagpipes are attested throughout medieval Europe and an English set is mentioned in *The Canterbury Tales* (1380). The first clear reference to Scottish pipes is not until the 16th century.

Cardiff: Here's a bit of geography that'll blow your mind. The Welsh capital is farther east than Edinburgh. Let that sink in … We tend to think of Britain as a craggy rectangle, whose main axis runs north–south. But that's not the case. The landmass has a distinctly westward tilt. So much so that the Scottish capital, though toward the east coast of Scotland, is ever so slightly further west than the Welsh capital. Have a look on a map if you don't believe me. By the same token, Southampton is farther east than Newcastle and mainland Scotland is entirely west of Oxford.

Forth Bridge: 'It's like the painting of the Forth Bridge.' This common cliché suggests a time-consuming task that, once complete, must be started all over again. It's a modern take on the labours of Sisyphus, condemned to push a boulder up a hill only for it to roll back down again, for eternity. Likewise, the Forth Bridge near Edinburgh is so immense that as soon as it has been coated in paint, it's time to repaint the first sections again. The notion was never quite correct. The bridge did require near-constant touch-ups, but maintenance crews focused on the most weathered parts rather than systematically renewing the coating. Since 2011 the cliché is well and truly outmoded. A new type of epoxy paint now covers the span, and should last a quarter-century without renewal. 'Like painting the Forth Bridge' may come to represent something that happens once a generation.

Giant's Causeway: Northern Ireland's most famous landmark is a spit of rock jutting out into the North Channel from County Antrim. The so-called Giant's Causeway is supposed in myth to be the work of a giant called Finn MacCool. The oversized labourer built a bridge to Scotland so he could fight a rival giant. The stone causeway was actually created by lava flow some 50–60 million years ago, just after Earth's true giants, the dinosaurs, had been wiped out by another big rock. As seaside features go, it's hardly a whopper. Neighbouring fingers of rock jut out further into the sea, and some visitors are surprised at the less-than-gigantic scale. Rather, its fame rests on the constituent 40,000 polygonal blocks, mostly hexagonal, that look almost artificial. Their formation is now understood by geologists, but the sight is nevertheless impressive. The columns are by no means unique – similar formations are found at Fingal's Cave across the water in Scotland, and helped contribute to the Giant's Causeway legend. Hundreds of other examples are known around the world.

Haggis: Sheep's lungs, heart and liver, oatmeal, suet, onion and spices served in an animal's stomach. The traditional Scottish haggis is beyond many people's 'yuck' threshold, though those who try it are seldom disappointed. Like many other foodstuffs associated with a particular region (see Cornish pasties and Shropshire Blue, for example), the haggis has debatable origins. Certainly, haggis-like dishes are attested from many cultures, going back to the ancient Greeks and Romans. Offal spoils quickly. Wrapping it in the stomach and boiling must have occurred to hunters millennia ago. How the basic recipe developed into the modern Scottish dish is a debate of intestinal circuitousness, with possible contributions from French, Danish and English kitchens. The Scottish have made the haggis their own, but its origins are not strictly Caledonian.

Scotch: A term to describe items associated with Scotland (Scotch whisky, Scotch bonnet, Scotch mist, etc.), but never people. Do so at your peril. Incidentally, the Scotch egg has little to do with Scotland. It was invented in the London department store Fortnum & Mason in 1738. The reasons for the name are debatable, but it may be derived from the verb 'scotched', meaning tampered with.

Tartan: Received wisdom would have us believe that each Scottish clan has its own tartan (or plaid, to our North American friends). A thread of truth meanders through the idea, but it is buried in a weft of romanticism. Criss-crossed woollens are an ancient part of Gaelic culture and have been worn in Scotland since time immemorial. The earliest known pattern (technically a 'sett') is from the 3rd century CE. Particular setts may have been popular in certain regions, but these depended on which natural dyes were available, and the whims of the weaver. Clan affiliation didn't play a large part.

Our modern associations with tartans began in the mid-18th century and grew from a number of influences. Tartans were outlawed in 1746 in a bid to stamp out uprisings in the Highlands. An exception was made for British soldiers in the Highland regiments. The military being the military, these soldiers were given a standardized tartan as part of their uniform. As new regiments were created, new tartans were introduced to differentiate them. The ban on civilian tartans was lifted in 1782. From this time, the association with clans began to grow. Many new patterns were introduced and ascribed to Scottish families – often to cultivate an identity rather than out of any historical basis. The writings of Sir Walter Scott and James Macpherson added new layers of romanticism to the dress.

The trend developed into a craze with the visit of George IV to Scotland in 1822, again egged on by Sir Walter Scott. From this point, tartan was seen as the national dress of Scotland, not restricted to the Highlands. Soon, Caledophiles everywhere could buy books of 'authentic' clan tartans, most of which had been invented in the early 19th century. The craze was further stoked by Queen Victoria and Prince Albert, whose long stays at Balmoral in Aberdeenshire made tartan dress and decoration deeply fashionable.

New setts have appeared ever since. Most readers will be familiar with the beige and red 'Burberry check' – an English invention from the 1920s. Many of the US States have official tartans, none of which existed before 1988. In 2012 the City of London registered its own tartan – a sober affair of greys and white criss-crossed with the red bands of St George. The name, incidentally, is of French origin. It is derived from *tiretaine*, a word meaning 'coarse, strong fabric'.

Welsh rabbit: A dish best described as glorified cheese-on-toast, Welsh rabbit contains no rabbit, and may not be Welsh. The name's origins are lost in the mists of time, though it is possible that Welsh simply means 'foreign' rather than a literal reference to that nation. The dish was commonly spelled as 'rabbit' until recent times. 'Rarebit' is now more usual, and less of an affront to the Trade Descriptions Act.

Whisky/whiskey: With an 'e' is the common spelling in Ireland, while without an 'e' is preferred in Scotland. Always remember this rule, because you'll get throttled by a pedant if you ever get it the wrong way around. The name, incidentally, comes from Gaelic *uisce* (or *uisge*) *beatha*, meaning 'water of life'.

Are you pronouncing it wrong?

Beaulieu: The Hampshire home of the British Motor Museum carries a conspicuously French look, but not pronunciation. Locals call it 'Bew-lee'. Curiously, much of the local land was once owned by Thomas Wriothesley, whose name is pronounced 'Risley'. Hampshire, abbreviated to Hants., is clearly England's most contrarian county.

Belvoir Castle: This famous Leicestershire Castle carries a name that can be traced back to the Norman invasion a millennium ago. Again, we don't pronounce it the French way. Instead, it is uttered like the furry mammal: 'Beaver' Castle.

Berkeley (and Berkshire): Here we have a transatlantic divergence that often causes confusion. Americans like their Berkeley (California) with a 'Burk', whereas Brits plump for a 'Bark'. In the interests of research, I spent a melodic half-hour going through every rendition of 'A Nightingale Sang in Berkeley Square' on Spotify. The titular square is in London, England, so should be pronounced 'Bark-ly'. And it is, even by American singers.

Bicester: The 'cester', 'chester' or 'caster' ending is common in English place names. It usually denotes a settlement built on a Roman fortress town. Hence, Leicester, Winchester, Manchester and the rest. Bicester has gained increased fame in recent years thanks to its designer outlet shopping centre which, for some reason, attracts visitors from all over the world. Many get the name wrong. It's pronounced 'Biss-ter', not 'Bi-sesster' or 'Bick-ester'.

Cholmondeley: Chances are you'll never visit Cholmondeley in Cheshire, perhaps the most obscure location on this list. I include it for the prolix spelling. It's simply 'Chum-ly'. More than half of the letters are redundant.

Cirencester: Unlike Bicester, Gloucester, Leicester and other places with this ending, which all abbreviate the 'cester' to a 'ster' sound, Cirencester does its own thing. It's pronounced 'Siren-sesster', and not 'Sirenster', as might be expected.

Ely: The tiny but beautiful city in Cambridgeshire is said as 'Eely', rather than 'Ellie'. The pronunciation reflects its possible (though disputed) etymology as a 'district of eels'.

Gloucester: Another old Roman name, Gloucester acts like Leicester and effectively harbours a silent 'ce'. Pronounce it 'Gloss-ster'.

Keighley: The small Yorkshire town has attracted wider fame thanks to its associations with the Brontë sisters. The temptation is to say 'Keely', but it's better to imagine a 't' in there and call it 'Keith-ly'.

Leicester: Often mangled as 'Lie-sesster', the Midlands city and the central London square are both pronounced as 'Less-ter'.

Magdalene College: Both Oxford and Cambridge universities are home to colleges dedicated to Mary Magdalene, both traditionally pronounced 'Maudleyn'. In Cambridge's case, the name was once written that way too, as an egotistical pun honouring Thomas Audley, who re-founded the college in 1542. The Oxford college is spelled without an 'e' (Magdalen), but also plumps for the 'Maudlin' sound. Meanwhile, Caius College in Cambridge is pronounced as 'Kees'.

Mousehole: A small Cornish town with a most curious name (it probably has nothing to do with mice, and may be a corrupted form of a Celtic phrase for a 'young woman's brook'). The pronunciation also shies away from the murine. Locals say 'Mow-zell', with the 'Mow' rhyming with 'cow'.

Salisbury: The important thing to remember here is that the 'i' is silent. The cathedral city is known as 'Salz-bree'.

Shrewsbury: Shropshire's county town often befuddles: is it 'Shrows-bury' or 'Shroos-bury'? Both are commonly heard. Even locals are equivocal. A 2015 poll by the *Shropshire Star* found 81 per cent plumping for the 'Shroo'. 'Shrow' has historical form; the Anglo-Saxon name for the town was Scrobbesburh, later corrupted to Schrosberie. But it seems the modern spelling has influenced speech patterns to favour 'Shroos-bury'.

Teignmouth: The Devon resort is quite simply pronounced as 'Tin-m'th', not 'Tain-mouth'.

Worcestershire: Everyone from visiting Americans to the titular ogre in *Shrek the Third* has trouble with this English county. Most Brits will be confident – the name is familiar not only from maps but also from the eponymous sauce. It should be pronounced 'Wuss-ter-sher', not 'Worce-ter-shy-er' (and note the ending; the English tend not to fully enunciate 'shire' when it's on the end of a county name, though we would for a shire horse. I do not know why). Other meddlesome counties include Berkshire ('Bark-sher'), Gloucestershire ('Gloss-ter-sher'), Leicestershire ('Less-ter-sher') and Warwickshire ('Wor-ick-sher').

Other myths and misnomers

British accent: There isn't one. Listen to a teenager from Romford and a pensioner from Dudley and they might be speaking different languages. Despite the homogenizing influences of mass media, Britain remains a country of regional dialects and accents.

County flags: The Cornish are proud of their flag. The black and white cross of St Piran can be spied all across the county, flying from buildings, enriching car bumpers and even gracing the packaging of Ginsters pasties. Its recorded history, however, is not as ancient as one might imagine. The first reference comes from an 1838 history of Cornwall, while the oldest surviving example can be seen in an 1888 stained-glass window at Westminster Abbey commemorating Cornish industrial hero Richard Trevithick. Even so, this is positively wizened compared to other county flags. All but three of the historic counties have official flags registered with the Flag Institute. (Hampshire, Herefordshire and Leicestershire are the odd ones out, in case you're wondering.) Of the 36 historic counties who do possess a standard, 25 were invented in the 21st century. The most recent, Suffolk and Oxfordshire, were registered as recently as October 2017. Both were, though, based on traditional emblems. My favourite has to be the flag of Wiltshire, made official in 2009. Its green and white stripes are superintended by a great bustard, an unfortunately named bird that was once extinct in England but has now been reintroduced to Wiltshire.

Duchy of Cornwall: A title held by the eldest son (but not daughter) of the reigning monarch. The privilege comes with a lot of land – 135,000 acres (54,633ha) – but only a small fraction is in Cornwall. About half the estate is in Devon, with further land in Cornwall, Herefordshire, Somerset and most of the Isles of Scilly.

Dungeness: Has nothing to do with dungeons. The Kentish protuberance gets its name from the Danish *nes* for 'headland', coupled with either an individual's name (Mr Denge), or a term meaning dangerous. I've included this remote land because of its reputation as the only desert in the country. The shingle beach at Dungeness is so windswept, barren and dry that it should be classed alongside the Sahara and Gobi. So goes the story, played out over a thousand web pages. But the facts are built on shifting sand. Dungeness receives copious rainfall – like anywhere in Britain. Its barren aspect is caused by high sea winds and saline conditions rather than a lack of precipitation. It is not, technically, a desert.

Ethelred the Unready: English monarchs get away with it lightly when it comes to nicknames. Bulgaria had a tsar called Ivaylo the Cabbage. Louis V of France was known as 'the Sluggard'. Castile had Henry the Impotent. The English Ethelred the Unready, who ushered in the second millennium as king of the English, still raises a smirk, however. The apparent lack of preparedness sounds comical to the modern ear. The epithet originally had a slightly different meaning. Unready, in a medieval sense, suggested one who was ill-advised rather than unprepared. The sobriquet probably arose as a satirical pun on Ethelred's name, which translates as 'well-advised'. It was not recorded until 150 years after his death, and was probably not used in his own lifetime. His predecessor King Edgar the Peaceful (c.943–75) also has a dubious nickname. This is the monarch who reputedly drove a javelin through the stomach of his love rival while on a hunting trip.

Great Train Robbers: Not that great. In August 1963, a gang of 16 men made off with £2.6 million from a Royal Mail train in Buckinghamshire. The crime is among the most audacious and famous in English history. Even so, nine of the men were captured within weeks due to their own stupidity. Few of the robbers got to spend any of their looted cash and those who did used most of it up in evading the authorities.

Greenwich Mean Time: Not necessarily the time in Greenwich. Thanks to daylight saving, the whole of the UK shifts an hour forward every spring. This puts the nation (even those in Greenwich) on British Summer Time (GMT+1), rather than Greenwich Mean Time.

I wandered lonely as a cloud ...: Perhaps the best-known poem about the English countryside was penned by William Wordsworth around 1805. Wordsworth wasn't lonely at all when he dreamt up that line. The poem was inspired by a walk with his sister Dorothy, during which they stumbled across a bright patch of daffodils.

Keep Calm and Carry On: A message intimately associated with the Second World War, but little seen at the time. A poster carrying this message was produced in 1939 to prepare the country for inevitable air raids. Some 2.5 million copies were printed, but only a handful were ever displayed. Those who did spot the posters often found them patronizing or humorous. One shopper in Cardiff in December 1940 was amused to see the sign in a shop window after he'd been turned away from the tills, purchase incomplete, due to an air-raid siren. The now famous phrase only came to prominence in the 21st century after a cache of the posters was rediscovered in an Alnwick bookshop in 2000. With its message of stiff upper lip and business as usual, it struck a chord with customers. The phrase is now a staple of greeting cards, fridge magnets and T-shirts.

Leeds Castle: Leeds is one of the most populous, important cities of northern England. Leeds Castle, a popular visitor attraction, is a four-hour drive away in deepest Kent. The two are entirely unconnected. The castle takes its name from the nearby village of Leeds, not the more famous northern city.

'M': The one thing anybody knows about the secret services is that they are secret ... and that they fulfil services, though quite what those services are is also a secret. MI6, the foreign intelligence service, is just one strand within this web of secrecy. Its spider – to push the metaphor – is well-known from the James Bond movies as 'M', most recently portrayed by Dame Judi Dench and Ralph Fiennes. Their real-world equivalent, though, is known as 'C' in honour of the first director of the secret services Captain Sir Mansfield George Smith-Cumming. The Captain was an eminently sensible man*. Rather than sign his abundant name in full, he instead scratched a 'C' for Cumming. The tradition was maintained by his successors. The moniker of 'M' was the invention of Bond author Ian Fleming, who simply used one of the many other initials enjoyed by Captain Sir MGS-C. The name 'MI6' is also a little dodgy. The organization's official name is the Secret Intelligence Service (SIS), with MI6 used colloquially.

Middlesex: Does Middlesex still exist? I once got roasted for suggesting the county had been abolished in the 1960s, subsumed into Greater London. I compared Middlesex to Diagon Alley in the Harry Potter films. If you know where to look, truly believe and wish hard enough, then Middlesex can be conjured into existence. Otherwise, it's a defunct, moribund, non-existent county.

Not so, claim its supporters. Middlesex County Council might have been abolished, and with it the administrative borders, but the name lingers on. Importantly, the Post Office continued to use Middlesex as a postal county for many years after the switch. The anachronism continued until 1996 when counties were dropped altogether from the mail delivery system. People still write, for example, 'Ruislip, Middlesex' rather than 'Ruislip, Greater London'. Middlesex still appears on old signposts, and in the name of the famous cricket club. Though it is absent from the political map, Middlesex survives still as an historic county of cultural importance.

---

* FOOTNOTE: I say that, but this is a man famous for stabbing himself in the leg with a paper knife during dull meetings. His leg was fake, unbeknown to those at the table.

Morris dancing: A stalwart of English fetes, morris dancing has uncertain origins. It may be a Spanish import, arriving on our shores in the Middle Ages as Moorish dancing. Because nobody knows for sure where it comes from, confusion reigns over the capitalization of the name. Some hold that it should be written morris dancing, just as disco dancing or salsa dancing would not expect a capital. But the temptation is there, not least because Morris is also a male name, which would take a capital. If the dance really does derive from Moorish traditions, then it does deserve a big 'M' but, in the absence of proof, either is acceptable.

The New Forest: New York got its moniker in 1664 when New Amsterdam was captured by the English. The word 'New' is a bit of a stretch for those 350-year-old place names, but this is nothing compared to the New Forest. The woody region, which stretches across Hampshire and Wiltshire has carried the adjective for nearly 1,000 years. It was William the Conqueror who provided the name, when he declared the area a royal forest around 1079. And, lo, it crops up in Domesday Book as *Nova Foresta*. Curiously, the forest claimed the lives of two of William's sons – Prince Richard and William II – perhaps divine retribution for the Conqueror's appropriation of the land.

Postage stamps and treason: Another common entry in articles about 'zany unrepealed laws' would have us believe that a poorly positioned stamp can land you in jail. It is apparently unlawful to place a postage stamp upside down, and such a wanton insult to the monarch can be considered treasonous. As a former scientist, I put my liberty at risk to test this one out. Reader, I can confirm that an envelope with an upended stamp will get to its destination unhindered. No questions asked. The threat of treason is a myth, with no basis in law. And I'd like to leave you with a bonus fact about stamps. The reigning monarch is always depicted facing left. On coins, however, the orientation of the august countenance has for centuries alternated between reigns. Queen Elizabeth II faces right, while her father gazed left.

Queen Victoria: The maudlin monarch* was not born with the name by which we all know her. She was Christened Alexandrina, but chose her second name upon her accession. Were it not for that personal whim, we might now talk about the Alexandrinian era or visit the Alexandrina and Albert Museum in London. Her son Edward VII followed suit. Known while heir apparent as Prince Albert Edward – or 'Bertie' to his inner circle – he chose Edward VII as his regnal name. This he did in deference to his father, ensuring that the long-dead Prince Consort would remain the only royal Albert. Edward's grandson George VI was the last to reign under a changed name. He too was an Albert, Prince Albert Frederick Arthur George. The first three names were spurned in favour of George. The current Prince of Wales has indicated that he might like to be known as George upon his own accession, though given that he's already 70, King Methuselah might be more appropriate.

Sherlock Holmes: The icon of English crime fiction never uttered the line 'Elementary my dear Watson,' at least not in Arthur Conan Doyle's 'canonical' stories. The author uses the word 'elementary' on eight occasions and the phrase 'my dear Watson' 83 times, but never the

---

* FOOTNOTE: Who never, incidentally, said 'We are not amused' on record.

twain do meet. The now iconic phrase is a later mutation, first used on the stage and screen. The deerstalker hat and curving pipe are also later twists on the character. And here's a bonus fact I uncovered, while mapping every location in every story: Holmes and Watson visit some rather obscure bits of London, from Norwood to Chislehurst, but they never once set foot in Soho, just a 10-minute walk from their home on Baker Street.

Stiff upper lip: The true Englishman, so it was once said, should always keep a stiff upper lip. The phrase is supposed to convey focus, steadfastness and an unflappable resolve in the face of pressure. No emotion must be shown. A man must be a man, and never betray his fears to others. It is the wounded soldier who refuses to give up his position; the Captain going down with his ship; the embattled father trapped in a toddlers' party. It is almost always a male stereotype – one that is now dissolving, and perhaps for the better – and usually applied to British, specifically English men. Strange then, that the phrase was coined in the USA. Examples can be found as far back as 1815, but the first unambiguous use of the term in its current sense dates from the *Huron Reflector* (a newspaper, not a telescope) of 1830. The phrase was also used by Davy 'King of the Wild Frontier' Crockett in his 1834 autobiography – and it doesn't get much more American than that.

Thomas à Becket: The murdered Archbishop of Canterbury, turned saint and martyr is probably the most famous Englishman of the 12th century, royalty excepted. His name has always bugged me. What's with that 'à' between his names? Was he from a place called 'Becket'? Not directly. Thomas was born on Cheapside in London, opposite St Mary-le-Bow (famous church of Cockneys), though his ancestors may have been from Bec Abbey in Normandy. The 'à' is ahistorical. Nobody called him that at the time, and it's not until the Tudor period, 400 years later, that someone thought to add the French à to denote 'from'. While I wouldn't be so harsh as to say Thomas à Becket is 'wrong', the middle bit is unnecessary, especially in this modern age where to type an accented letter seems such a chore.

Let's start a new wave of false facts

Having debunked so many English myths and stereotypes, it's time to replace them with some new ones. The following are all made up. Please help spread them as fact so, 100 years from now, somebody else can write a sequel to this book.

* Until the M1 motorway was built, the chasm known as the Watford Gap was all but impassable. Motorists faced a 16km (10 mile) round-trip via Northampton.

* Scones were given their name in honour of the Stone of Scone. They are equally hard and unpalatable.

* The River Severn was named by Roman soldiers, as the Seventh Legion made their main camp at Gloucester. In a similar way the Trent and Derwent are both corruptions of 'Twentieth', for the legion based in the East Midlands. The Rivers Avon and Exe have more convoluted etymologies, but essentially take their names from the fifth (V) and tenth (X) legions. An estimated two-thirds of English rivers were named in this way.

* Until the 1950s, the English spelled lobster as lobcester.

* There are no hedgehogs in the county of Rutland, and nobody knows why.

* Thanks to an unrepealed law, it is an offence to ride a donkey on Cleethorpes beach, or even to watch somebody else ride a donkey on Cleethorpes beach, unless the donkey is shod in boots.

* When examined up close, the White Cliffs of Dover are really a dirty cream colour, like cappuccino. They only appear white thanks to refraction of the Sun's rays in the sea spray.

* Cornwall gets its name from a long-lost Roman fortification akin to Hadrian's Wall, but made from hay bales as a cost-saving measure.

* Thanks to Brexit and the repeal of European legislation, it is once again legal for an Englishman to shoot a Scotsman from the walls of York.

* The City of London is England's smallest city. However, if you include all the floor space in its many skyscrapers, it would cover an area the size of Hampshire.

* The government has secret plans to relocate Parliament to Bedfordshire in 2030 when London is expected to succumb to a combination of widespread subsidence and rising sea levels. Bedfordshire was chosen because of the inland location and the convenience of Luton airport.

* Walkers tackling the gruelling trek from Land's End to John o' Groats should consider tackling it the other way around. Because of the curvature of the Earth, the trek is largely downhill when accomplished from north to south.

Index

Acknowledgements

I'd like to thank Mark Mason and Martin Davies for helpful suggestions. The British Newspaper Archive was indispensable for digging up some long-lost details on numerous stories.

About the author

Matt Brown has been writing professionally about London and England for more than a decade, and serves as Editor at Large of Londonist.com. He's visited every county and lived in five of them (six if we allow the continued existence of Middlesex). Matt is the author of six other Everything You Know books, including London, Science, Art, Space, the Human Body and Planet Earth.

Other titles in the series

Everything You Know
About London is
Wrong
9781849943604

Everything You Know
About Science is
Wrong
9781849944021

Everything You Know
About Art is
Wrong
9781849944298

Everything You Know
About Space is
Wrong
9781849944304

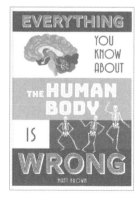

Everything You Know
About The Human
Body is Wrong
9781849944311

Everything You Know
About Planet Earth is
Wrong
9781849944540